Holiness Revolution

DAN DEMATTE

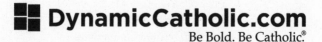

HOLINESS REVOLUTION

Printed in the United States of America. [1]

ISBN: 978-1-937509-30-9

Cover Design: Aaron Richards
Interior Design: Shawna Powell

Dynamic Catholic® and Be Bold. Be Catholic.®
and The Best Version of Yourself® are
registered trademarks of The Dynamic Catholic Institute.

For more information on this title
and other books and CDs available through
the Dynamic Catholic Book Program, please visit:
www.DynamicCatholic.com

The Dynamic Catholic Institute
5081 Olympic Blvd
Erlanger, Kentucky 41018
Phone: 1–859–980–7900
Email: info@DynamicCatholic.com

table of Contents

Part 3: the Revolution of the World

ALL FOR JESUS. ALL FOR HIS KINGDOM.

INTRODUCTION

A few months ago, I walked into a beat-up warehouse with a For Sale sign on it. I had been looking for a piece-of-junk building to do youth ministry out of and I was hopeful that the Lord would just give me this particular building. . . and so I entered. Inside I was greeted by a large beast of a man in his fifties. His dress was that of a dirty construction worker and hands were dried and cracked from a life of manual labor. In a deep, angry voice, he confronted me and asked me why I was there and what I was doing. I told him that I was a youth minister who was trying to start a revolution of holiness in the world and that I needed a building to gather the youth of Columbus, Ohio.

"Well, do you have any money?" he asked.

"No, but God has plenty of it, so I'm not worried about that," I replied.

He ignored my reply and looked at me with condescending eyes, followed by condescending words: "You're young. I bet you think you can change the world, don't you?"

I laughed. "No way! I don't think I can change the world, but I know God can."

His reply failed to take into account my answer. "Young kids always think they can change the world," he said. "I used to try to help people, but then I found out that they just take advantage of your help. People have been trying to change the world for years and the world still sucks. If you ask me, it's worse than ever."

Knowing he needed the hope of heaven, I responded to his pessimism: "Yeah, the world's pretty rough right now. Good thing we don't live for this world; we live for heaven. We're just here for a few passing years, but our ultimate hope is the hope of heaven."

Silence. Prompting him to reply, I asked, "Right?"

Lowering his head, he answered, "I don't know. All I know is that right now I'm just looking out for me. I'm losing my job today; tomorrow this warehouse will be closed and I and all the other employees are out of work."

I could say nothing more, and so I simply asked him if I could pray for him. I prayed with this man then and there, and I told him to trust in God no matter what.

What we all need right now is hope. In a world filled with empty promises that lead to despair and brokenness, we need to know that fulfillment can be found only in Jesus Christ. We need to place our hope and trust in Jesus and in his saving power. I want to see people who are alive in Christ — alive with his joy, alive with his zeal, alive with his mission of bringing all souls to the Father and ushering in the Kingdom of God. I want to see *you* living a life of passion and purpose, living the adventure that Christ is calling you to live!

We, the people of God in the third millennium, are living in an amazing time of salvation history. Pope Paul VI, Pope John Paul II, and Pope Benedict XVI have all prophetically spoken of a new Pentecost, a new evangelization, and a new springtime within the Church and throughout the world. They have all spoken and written words of hope and confidence in God. Now is the time for renewal! Now is the time for hope!

I don't believe that the end of the world is as near as some radical Christians shout. I believe renewal is near and that more great saints and martyrs are to come. I believe that the Holy Spirit is stirring up a mighty revolution in the minds and hearts of Catholics everywhere — a revolution that will not and cannot be silenced. And most of all, I believe that this renewal will come from the young Church. It is the youth of the Church who will set the world ablaze with the fire of God's love. We will not sit idle and watch this world reject Christ and the teachings of his Church. We will rise. Even if it is a small and weak group, we will rise. And we will rise triumphantly as Christ rose triumphant over sin and death more than two thousand years ago.

This book is meant to plant the seed of renewal within your heart. We have an amazing God who "makes all things new" (Revelation 21:5), and this amazing God wants to use you in his plan for renewal.

Even though he has the power to literally renew the face of the earth simply with the words from his mouth, he does not do so. Even though he has the power to renew the face of the earth with mighty winds and powerful forces, he does not do so. He chooses to use you and me — he wants to bring renewal *in* his people *through* his people.

So often I sit down with hopeless teenagers and hear them say that they don't believe in God because of all the pain and suffering in the world. If there really was an all-loving God, then why wouldn't he do something to stop all the hurt? The thing that these teenagers fail to see is that God is doing something about it. At every moment of every day, Jesus Christ is calling his disciples to be a light in the darkness, to be a source of renewal. He is doing something about the pain and the hurt — he is calling *you*, and he is calling you *today*.

The problem isn't that God is distant. The problem isn't that God fails to do anything to stop the pain and suffering in the world. The problem is that the people whom Christ calls are too busy with their own lives to answer his call. How can we focus on doing his will when we are so consumed with our own?

What will become of this world if the people of God do not answer his call?

What will become of this world if the people of God live in fear?

What will become of this world if the people of God sit around and do nothing?

"You are the light of this world. A city built on a hill cannot be hidden. Nor do they light a lamp and then put it under a bushel basket; it is set on a lampstand, where it gives light to all in the house. Just so, your light must shine before others, that they may see your good deeds and glorify your heavenly Father." (Matthew 5:14–16)

Stop wasting your life.

Do something amazing for the Gospel.

All for Jesus. All for his kingdom.

1 PETER 2:9-12 "But you are a chosen people, a royal priesthood, a holy nation, a people belonging to God, that you may declare the praises of him who called you out of darkness into his wonderful light. Once you were not a people, but now you are the people of God; once you had not received mercy, but now you have received mercy. Dear friends, I urge you, as aliens and strangers in the world, to abstain from sinful desires, which war against your soul. Live such good lives among the pagans that, though they accuse you of doing wrong, they may see your good deeds and glorify God on the day he visits us."

PART ONE:

THE
REVOLUTION
BEGINS

1
THE WAR AT HAND

"It is time, Father. We can wait no longer."

"It's foolishness! If you want to march out of this house to your death, and leave your mother without a son, then so be it; but mark my words, son, you will not receive my support."

"This hurts me deeply, Father. You are the one who taught me God created all men free, with certain rights that no one can take away. You are the one who taught me to stand up for my beliefs, no matter what the cost."

"But I also taught you how to think, and you aren't using your head. The militia is outnumbered six to one. You are untrained. You lack the experience. You haven't the right weapons for war."

"But if I don't fight, then who will?"

"Maybe this isn't your battle to fight. Maybe the battle has already been won by the enemy. Maybe it is time to stop this revolution and simply live the way the British want us to live."

"Or maybe it is time for young people like me to give their lives over to the cause of freedom so that this world can see a complete and radical change. And maybe, Father, just maybe, if enough of us give everything that we have, and enough of us quit counting the cost, then maybe the change isn't that far off. I will fight. I will not shrink back in fear."

One word began to ring within the hearts and minds of the young people of the early American colonies: *revolution*. England had crossed the line; they had charged one too many taxes, they had pushed one too many laws, and they had stolen one too many God-given freedoms. It was time for the colonists to rise up and bring about a radical change. **It was time for a revolution.** This revolution didn't come from an organized and systematic government; it came from an unorganized, unqualified group of young men who were willing to put everything on the line, without counting the costs.

A revolution is an uprising of people seeking to bring about a complete and radical change. A revolution starts in the minds and hearts of the people. It always comes from the bottom up, because it seeks to overthrow the authority that lays hold of the people, that is restricting their freedom.

Revolutions require much, demand much, and endure much. They require staking your entire life on your beliefs and letting nothing and no one stop you from the change you know is urgent. In order to win a revolution, one must never consider the odds or count the costs; one must simply put everything on the line at all times.

Imagine what our lives would be like if the colonists hadn't fought. Imagine what our country would look like if the militia had given up — if they had dropped their guns and ceased fighting because the odds weren't in their favor. Imagine if the young people who rose up to fight in the American Revolution had decided not to continue fighting because it may have resulted in their death or because it was too hard. The United States of America as we know it today would not exist. Because the militia was unwilling to allow things to remain the way they were, its soldiers fought and fought and fought, and they ultimately achieved the goal of all revolutions: freedom and change.

More than two hundred years ago, young people in this great nation placed their lives on the line while fighting the American Revolution. The result was our freedom. They made tremendous sacrifices, suffered agonizing pain, and died many sorrowful deaths —but they now share in an ongoing victory. The heart of the Revolution endured, the complete and radical change was accomplished, and the colonies proudly became the United States of America.

ARE WE ALL THAT DIFFERENT?

This question goes through my mind day and night. Are we Americans living in the twenty-first century much different from the American colonists? We are not. We have more in common with them than you could ever imagine.

If only the early American revolutionaries could see our country today. They would mourn. **We are not the land of the free and we definitely are not the home of the brave. We are slaves and we are cowards.**

Just think about the language of the Declaration of Independence for one moment: "We hold these truths to be self-evident, that all men are created equal, that they are endowed by their Creator with certain inalienable rights, that among these are life, liberty and the pursuit of happiness."

Now answer me this: Do we as Americans hold true that there is a Creator and that he is in charge, or have we made ourselves God? Do we see that all people have the right to life, from womb to tomb? Are we really free, or are we slaves to our own sinfulness and materialism? Does the current American culture really lead to happiness? Are you sincerely happy? Or are you longing for more?

This book isn't about a second American Revolution or overthrowing the American government; it is by no means political. I am convinced that the change this great country needs, and the change this world desperately needs, is one that cannot be accomplished by government officials.

The country and the world change when the people of God say it does. When the people of God cast away the

15

lies and corruption, that is when we will see change. Change does not come from a man. It does not come from a president. It comes from God, and God alone.

The Holy Father spoke these words in Cologne, Germany, at World Youth Day in 2005: "It is not ideologies that save the world, but only a return to the living God, our Creator, the guarantor of our freedom, the guarantor of what is really good and true. True revolution consists in simply turning to God, who is the measure of what is right and who at the same time is everlasting love. **And what could ever save us apart from love?"**

If we want to return to freedom, if we want to return to what is really good and true, and if we want to return to real happiness and real joy, then we *must* return to the living God. We must look to God who is love himself, and we must know him. We must know his ways, know his will, know his words. Christians and non-Christians alike have been trying to bring about reform for hundreds of years. They try to do good and fix society, but they do so relying on their own power and in their own name, as opposed to doing so with the power of almighty God and in the name above all names, the name of Jesus Christ our returning king.

Today, I challenge you to join a *new* American Revolution, a revolution of holiness, a revolution that comes from God! This revolution isn't about overthrowing a government. It's about overthrowing the authorities of sin and Satan that lay hold of all people. It's about overthrowing hearts that have not been won over by the great love of the Gospel, the love of Jesus Christ. It's about finding *real* happiness, seeking *true* freedom, and becoming *truly* brave. Then, and only then, will we be the land of the free and the home of the brave.

FREEDOM!

Revolutions take place because people want freedom. Freedom is why revolutions are begun, and freedom is why revolutions are won against all odds.

Today and all days I wake up and declare war. I declare war on the authorities that have caused so many Americans to become slaves. I **declare war** on the unseen principalities that are destroying the lives of those around me. Our revolution is not a war against a tyrannical government, but rather one against sin and Satan and all of his empty promises.

The war we wage is war against the materialism that consumes the hearts of men. It is a war against the relativism that declares that there are no moral truths. It is a war against the pluralism that declares there is no one religion that possesses the fullness of truth. It is a war against individualism, in which selfishness and egotism reign as god. It is a revolution against the culture of death that promotes abortion and contraception as good, seeking selfishness over the dignity of every human life. It is a war against all the social injustices of our times: racism, sexism, slavery, and on and on. It is a war fighting hard against the breakdown of marriage and family life, seeking to uphold *God's* design for marriage, between one man and one woman, until death do you part. It is a war against the filth of pornography the spread of premarital sex. It is a war against the horror of the sexual revolution, which has brought nothing but brokenness: broken hearts, broken homes, and broken love.

We have it far worse than the American colonists. While their freedom was restricted, at least they were not slaves. In the war we wage, we are slaves. Jesus says to us, "Everyone who sins is a slave to sin." (John 8:34) We are all bound by the chains of sin and we are all held captive to the Devil's empty promises. The more we as a people dwell in sin, the more we dwell in slavery.

Jesus says, "The thief comes to steal, slaughter and destroy, but I **have come so that you might have life,** life to the fullest." (John 10:10) We live in a corrupt generation in which the Devil seeks to steal, slaughter, and destroy God's plan for our happiness and our salvation. The Devil is destroying our lives, and instead of raising arms up against the enemy and fighting, we prefer things to remain the way they are, and share in the enemy's empty promises.

We are fools to buy into these empty promises. We are fools to think that sex and foreplay, drugs and alcohol, money and materialism, electronics and technology, selfishness and pride will ever make us happy. We think that if only we could become popular enough or start dating this particular person, if only we could afford these clothes, or get this grade point average, then finally we would be happy. But that is exactly what the enemy wants us to think. It is his goal to distract you from your destination; it is his goal to steal from you God's plan of happiness for your life.

I dare say that no sexual conquest, no material possession, no state championship, no college scholarship, no social status, no dream job, no amount of money will ever make you happy. **Nothing, nothing will make you happy other than the love of Jesus Christ.**

And so we find ourselves here in the twenty-first century at a time in which we are at war. **We are at war with sin and Satan, and all his empty promises.** It is up to us to decide whether or not we will rise up against the evil authority of sin that holds us captive and fight for freedom. **To be a Christian is to be a warrior.** To be a Christian is to be a fighter. Saint John Chrysostom accurately said, "We are baptized in order to fight!" It is time you and I start fighting. It is time you and I start a revolution in order to bring about a complete and radical change!

Our revolution is against the unseen principalities ruling over the minds and hearts of Americans: materialism, individualism, secularism, relativism, egotism, pride, lust, sloth, despair, anger, envy, and greed.

Saint Paul says, "Where the Spirit of the Lord is, there is freedom." (2 Corinthians 3:17b) And so let us call upon the Spirit of the Lord before we go any further.

Come, Holy Spirit. Come, great fire of God. Fill the hearts of thy faithful and enkindle in them the fire of your love. Send forth thy Spirit and they

shall be created. And you shall renew the face of the earth. Let us pray: O
God, who didst instruct the hearts of the faithful by the light of the Holy
Spirit, grant us in the same Spirit to be truly wise, and ever to rejoice in his
consolation through Christ our Lord. Amen.

It is the Spirit of God who brings freedom, and it is the Spirit of God who renews the face of the earth.

WHERE ARE THE BRAVE?

At what point in time did Christianity go from being a faith in which brave men and women were willing to die to being a wimpy spirituality based on mere emotions? In the early Church, if you were a Christian, you staked your life on your beliefs. Believing in the Triune God and the most holy Eucharist meant you could and most likely would be brutally murdered for your beliefs. That is why Christianity endured. Brave men and women believed **Christianity was worth living for – and worth dying for.**

But let me ask you this: How many American Catholics do you know who would be willing to die for their faith? For many, our faith is nothing more than a crutch we use to feel all warm and fuzzy inside. There's nothing warm and fuzzy about the Gospel. Jesus says, "Do not think that I have come to bring peace upon the earth. I have come to bring not peace, but the sword." (Matthew 10:34) The Gospel is intense. The Gospel is controversial. The Gospel requires the bravehearted.

One of my favorite scenes in Scripture comes when King David is on his deathbed having his last conversation with his son, Solomon. Solomon is to become the next King of Israel, a responsibility that is not the easiest task in the world. Israel had many enemies and waged many battles, and the king is the person who bravely leads his men into battle. Solomon, seeing his father dying, knows fully the responsibility that will soon be his: He will be leading armies into war. He will be following in his father's footsteps. Reading this, I picture one of the most moving moments in both of their lives, as David lies on his bed, Solomon kneeling near him timid with fear. The dying king takes Solomon's hand, looks his son deep in the eyes, and says, **Take courage, and be a man.** (1 Kings 2:2)

I feel as though we are all Solomon. We all kneel before our king, the king of kings and the lord of lords, Jesus Christ. We are afraid, and timid, and we know that living as a Christian in today's world is not easy, because the enemy is strong and fierce. We are busy counting the costs, calculating just how much we want to give to Christ ("I'll give him my Sunday mornings, and a few of my bad habits, but not everything"). We are afraid to give our life over to this revolution of holiness. We are afraid to war against the sin in our own life and in this corrupt generation. But our holy king takes our hand, looks us deep in the eyes, and utters this commission: "Take courage!"

Put on courage, young warrior!

"The hour has come for you to wake up from your slumber, because our salvation is nearer now than when we first believed. The night is nearly over; the day is almost here. So let us put aside the deeds of darkness and put on the armor of light." (Romans 13:11–12)

"Put off your old self, which is being corrupted by its deceitful desires; **to be made new** in the attitude of your minds; and put on the new self, created to be like God in true righteousness and holiness." (Ephesians 4:22–24)

"Finally, be strong in the Lord and in his mighty power. Put on the full armor of God so that you can take your stand against the devil's schemes. For our struggle is not against flesh and blood, but against the rulers, against the authorities, against the powers of this dark world and against the spiritual forces of evil in the heavenly realms. Therefore put on the full armor of God, so that when the day of evil comes, after you have done everything, you may be able to stand your ground." (Ephesians 6:10–13)

**Stop counting the costs. Give everything.
Join the Holiness Revolution.
Victory is ours!**

TALK ABOUT IT

(If reading with a group, use these questions for discussion.)

1. What is the darkness you see in the world?

2. Why are we slaves? What brings us freedom?

3. How would you describe the war we wage?

4. Are you free? Free to love? Free to live according to God's will? Why or why not?

5. What do you fear the most? Where do you need to be courageous?

6. Spend time reading and discussing the scriptures at the end of this chapter:

   a. Romans 13:11-12: Are you a sleeping Christian in need of waking up? Why or why not?

   b. Ephesians 4:22-24: What about the old self do you need to put off? What would your life look like if you were made new?

   c. Ephesians 6:10-13: What is the armor of God? What kind of armor would you like to ask him for?

7. Close your time together praying for each other in the areas you have discussed.

TAKE ACTION

ACTION STEP 1: Do two courageous things:

1. Seek someone out this week who is hurting or going through a hard time and ask if you can pray with them. Stop whatever you are doing and pray with and for that person.

2. Seek someone out this week who is hurting and tell them about Jesus' love. Share hope with them!

ACTION STEP 2: If you are reading this book alone, encourage a friend to read this book with you so that you have someone to talk to as you read.

ACTION STEP 3: Who are the people God has sent you to help you grow in your faith? Seek them out this week and thank them for their bravery in sharing the love of Jesus with others, especially you.

www.Holiness Revolution.com

2
THE HOLINESS REVOLUTION

On August 20, 2005, Pope Benedict stood in front of hundreds of thousands of Catholic teenagers at World Youth Day in Cologne, Germany, and declared that what the world needs right now is a spiritual revolution of holiness. Remember, a revolution is an uprising of people seeking to bring about a complete and radical change. And so a **Holiness Revolution is an uprising of Christian people seeking to bring about a complete and radical change in the world through holiness.**

True reform, true change, comes when the minds and hearts of people have been converted to the living God. **Conversion alone brings real reform.** So often, we spend countless hours trying to bring reform by imposing rules or laws, and we spend so little time striving to bring people into a relationship with Jesus Christ.

Our world is in dire need of a complete and radical change. Our world is in dire need of renewal. **Our world is in dire need of Jesus Christ.** You don't believe me? Wake up and open your eyes:

Every day in America:

- 6 teenagers commit suicide
- 200 teenagers are arrested
- 500 teenagers start doing drugs
- 1,000 teenagers start drinking alcohol
- 4,000 babies are murdered legally through abortion
- 8,000 teenagers become sexually active

Abortion Holocaust:

- Every day, 125,000 children are aborted throughout the world, totaling more than 45 million abortions every year.

- Almost every third child in America is killed through abortion.

- Every second of the day, 1.4 children are aborted.

Homelessness and Poverty:

- Every day, 30,000 children throughout the world die from the lack of food. That's nearly 11 million children a year.

- At least 80 percent of the world lives on less than $10 a day. (globalissues.org)

- Almost half of the world lives in severe poverty, living on less than $2 a day.

- 1.1 billion people in developing countries have inadequate access to water. (globalissues.org)

- 2.6 billion people in the world lack basic sanitation. (globalissues.org)

- In the United States 600,000 families and their 1.35 million children are homeless. (endhomelessness.org)

Slavery and Human Trafficking:

- 27 million people still live in slavery across the world. (Kevin Bales, Free the Slaves)

- Every year, 1 million children are exploited by the global commercial sex trade. (U.S. Department of State, "The Facts About Child Sex Tourism," 2005)

- The average age that children are first exploited through prostitution is 12. (humantrafficking.change.org)

- An estimated 200,000 American children are at risk for trafficking into the sex industry. (sctnow.org)

Pornography:

- The pornography industry makes nearly $100 billion every year. (http://internet-filter-review.toptenreviews.com/internet-pornography-statistics.html#anchor1)

- 2.5 million children are sexually exploited in the multibillion-dollar commercial sex industry. (sctnow.org)

- The average age of a child's first Internet pornography exposure is 11. (http://internet-filter-review.toptenreviews.com/internet-pornography-statistics.html#anchor1)

- 98% of men and 83% of women have been exposed to pornography. (myrocktoday.org)

- 50% of Christians say they struggle with pornography. (http://internet-filter-review.toptenreviews.com/internet-pornography-statistics.html#anchor1)

Domestic Problems in America:

- Nearly 50% of marriages end in divorce.

- About 60% of men and 40% of women will have an affair at some point in their marriage. (*The Monogamy Myth,* Peggy Vaughan)

- Every day, 4 to 5 children die in America as a result of child abuse. Most are under the age of 4. (childhelp.org)

- More than 3 million reports of child abuse are made every year in the United States. (childhelp.org)

Still not convinced that the world is in dire need of a complete and radical change? Think about all the rest of the darkness looming in the world that is difficult to measure:

- war, terrorism, bomb threats, genocide, racism

- hate groups, crime, robbery
- murders, beatings, gangs
- stress, anxiety, depression
- eating disorders, self-cutting, suicide
- drugs, alcohol, gambling
- distrust, resentment, envy
- bullying, lying, cheating

I can't help but look at these statistics and cry out to Jesus for renewal. I can't help but beg him to help us. I meet kids and adults from all over the country and I learn one thing: They are hurting. Everywhere I go I run into people who are hurting. There is a lot that is messed up in this world, and there are so many victims. People search and search for love and happiness but never find it. They long for hope, while they struggle in misery. They seek joy, but end up finding despair.

God has given us a great voice to speak to the hearts of this world, the voice of our Holy Father, Pope Benedict XVI. With great humility, the Holy Father knows and sees the grave injustices of the world, and he tells us this:

"To all of you I appeal: **Open wide your hearts to God!** Let yourselves be surprised by Christ! Open the doors of your freedom to his merciful love! Share your joys and pains with Christ, and let him enlighten your minds with his light and touch your hearts with his grace.

"Dear young people, **the happiness you are seeking, the happiness you have a right to enjoy, has a name and a face: It is Jesus of Nazareth, hidden in the Eucharist.** Only he gives the fullness of life to humanity! With Mary, say your own yes to God, for he wishes to give himself to you."

(Welcoming Celebration, World Youth Day, Cologne, Germany)

"If we let Christ into our lives, we lose nothing, nothing, absolutely nothing of what makes life free, beautiful, and great. No! Only in this friendship are the doors of life opened wide. Only in this friendship is the great potential of human existence truly revealed. Only in this friendship do we experience beauty and freedom." (Homily at the Mass of Inauguration, April 24, 2005)

"In these days **I encourage you to commit yourselves without reserve to serving Christ, whatever the cost.** The encounter with Jesus Christ will allow you to experience in your hearts the joy of his living and life-giving presence and enable you to bear witness to it before others." (Welcoming Celebration, World Youth Day)

The problems of the world seem overbearing. They seem impossible to change and to overcome. But we have found the answer to these problems. **The answer is Jesus.** For he is the one who will make *everything* new (Revelation 21:3–5). And if we have the answer to all of the world's pain and all of the world's suffering, if we have the answer to the world's emptiness, the world's longing, then what are we doing about it?

Once again, our Holy Father, drawing us deep into the heart of Jesus, commissions us to bring Christ to the world and to renew and reform the world through the holiness of God.

"Anyone who has discovered Christ must lead others to him. A great joy cannot be kept to oneself. It has to be passed on." (Benedict XVI, Mass in Marienfeld, Cologne, Germany, 2005)

"Today it is your task, dear young people, to live and breathe the Church's universality. Let yourselves be inflamed by the fire of the Spirit, so that a new Pentecost may be created among you and renew the Church." (Cathedral Mass, World Youth Day, 2005)

SHINE LIKE THE STARS IN THIS CORRUPT AND DEPRAVED GENERATION. (PHILIPPIANS 2:15)

We live in a culture of death. We live in a world that needs men and women who are willing to rise up and bring about a complete and radical change. We need rebels. We need true revolutionaries.

It is no longer rebellious to drink and have sex. It is no longer rebellious to cuss and disrespect authority. It is no longer rebellious to sin and live in darkness. Sin is not rebellion; it is conformity. If you're steeped in materialism, selfishness, and sin, you are just a conformist. If you want to be a rebel, if you want to be a revolutionary, you need to be a saint. **The saints are the real rebels** — they are the ones doing what no one else is doing. In this corrupt generation, it's rebellious to go to daily mass, to read your Bible, to live virtuously, to defend the truth, and to live in the light. That's rebellion!

I'm not a pessimist. But I am real and honest. My eyes have been opened by the light of the Holy Spirit and when I look at this world, I don't see the Kingdom of God. I don't see a world thriving in Christian love and virtue. I see a world plagued deeply with sin and hatred. I see a world where we kill unborn children because we don't want the inconvenience of them in our lives. I see a world where sex and marriage has been changed from something sacred into a recreational sport promoting pleasure and selfishness above holiness and sacrifice. I see a world where people are hurting, and instead of loving them, we add to their pain. I see a world where people are starving to death while others are dying of obesity. I see a world where the poor man gets rejected, the elderly woman gets ignored, and the child is left to raise himself. I see a world where man makes himself a god, and God becomes an inconvenience. I see a world worshipping money and possessions more than God. I see a world where silence is feared and noise pollutes our minds and hearts such that we never hear the voice of God. **I see a world of "Christians" who live more like the Pharisees than like Christ.** I see a world of "nice" people who defend tolerance more than they defend the dignity of every human life. I see a world where *everything* is *tolerated* except for truth and morality. If this is not a corrupt and depraved generation, my friends, then I don't know what is!

When we pray the Our Father, we pray, "Thy kingdom come, thy will be done, on earth as it is in heaven." Our call as Christians, and our pledge to God the Father in this prayer, is to shine like a star striving to transform this corrupt and depraved generation more into the image of the Kingdom of God. **If you pray this prayer but live a passive and dull Christian life, then you pray in vain.** The call of the Christian is to radically live the adventure of faith such that you work with Jesus Christ in bringing about the Kingdom of God here and now. But instead, when I think of Christians, I often think of people who live for a "convenient" Jesus, who are Christian for their own sake and not for the sake of the Kingdom of God.

Saint Paul says, "Do not present the parts of your bodies to sin as weapons of wickedness, but present yourselves to God as weapons for righteousness." (Romans 6:13) **You will never experience the fullness of the Christian life if it's all about you.** If you are a Christian for your own sake, then you've missed the mark. Yes, Christ suffered and died for you so that you might have eternal life, but he wants you to offer your body now as a weapon of righteousness. God wants you to live your life for the good of building up his kingdom.

Are we, the Christian people of America, really offering our bodies as weapons for righteousness? I'd say that some are, while many are not. I'd say that instead of living the Christian life of discipleship, many of us are sleeping. How can we sit and watch TV or YouTube videos for hours each week and waste so much time on meaningless social networks while the souls around us are rushing down the road to destruction? How can we have the nerve to say, 'I'm bored,' knowing that every single weekend thousands of people are trying to find happiness in sex, drugs, and alcohol? How can we be bored when every day thirty thousand children starve to death and 125,000 babies are aborted? **If you're bored, do something about the pain in the world!**

People are drowning in lives of meaninglessness and empty promises, and we have the answer. We know that it is Jesus that they seek and *we do nothing about it!* The tactic of the Devil is to get the fight out of us Christians. He wants to make us passive and passionless. He wants to crush the weapons of righteousness. He wants to rob you of your passion and zeal for the Gospel. If you aren't passionate for the full and abundant life of Christ and if you aren't passionate about sharing this life with everyone you meet, then the Spirit of God is not alive in you; the Spirit of God lies dormant in your life.

"Awake! Awake! Put on your strength O Zion." (Isaiah 52:1) **Wake up, you sleeping Christians!** Wake Up! Wake up, you sleeping dead, and experience the life of the Holy Spirit. Wake up and experience the full and abundant life of Christian discipleship, in which you live for something more important than your degree or your job, your pride or your sloth, your lust or your ego, your image or your possessions. In Christianity, you **live for something greater than yourself.** In Christ, you live for something eternal. You live for the kingdom. You live for the king.

All for Jesus! All for his kingdom!

"Awake, O Sleeper, rise to life. Christ is calling your name!" (Ephesians 5:14)

DO NOT LIVE FOR THIS WORLD

Ultimately, the world promises you everything but gives you nothing. And so I urge you, my brothers and sisters, quit living for this world. "Do not conform yourselves to this world, but rather, be transformed by the renewal of your mind so that you may do what is the will of God." (Romans 12:2) The way I see it, you have two options:

Either you will change the world, or the world will change you. What will it be?

The Holiness Revolution is about bringing a complete and radical change in the world. It's about serving God rather than serving yourself, about loving Jesus more than you love your sin. It's about rejecting sin and Satan, and living the radical life of a saint. It's a life of sacrifice. It's the Christian life.

If we live for this world, we will surely find ourselves at death's door, feeling empty, alone, and lost.

In high school I thought I had it all. I was well liked by my peers, dated a lot of good-looking girls, was the captain of the wrestling team, and held a 4.14 GPA at one of the toughest schools in the state. I was a "good kid" who didn't get into a lot of trouble, went to church and youth group, and was involved in a lot of extracurriculars. I dreamed of being great — but most of all, I dreamed that I would reach my two goals: going to the state championship in wrestling and getting into the University of Notre Dame. It was in fulfilling these dreams that I thought I would ultimately be happy.

I lived for this world and everything that I did was aimed at achieving these dreams. Surely, I thought, my hard work would make my dreams come true.

After four years of intense work in high school, my senior year came. I was ranked high in the state for wrestling, and I had a transcript stacked with all kinds of credentials that cried that I deserved to get into Notre Dame.

As you can probably guess, my dreams were not achieved. At the district meet for wrestling, I lost (to a guy I had beaten by fifteen points earlier in the season) because I accidently hit an illegal move. I didn't even make it to the state tournament. It wasn't but two weeks later that a letter from Notre Dame came in the mail. As I ripped open the envelope and sat on my couch, I read the words "While we were very impressed by your transcript, we regret to inform you that you have not been accepted to the University of Notre Dame." Even though I had a 4.14 GPA and a 32 on my ACT, I had been rejected . . . and rejected is how I felt.

My past burdens may seem trivial compared with yours, but what I learned stands true for all people. For years I had placed my identity in what I did and measured my happiness based on my success and failure. But at this point in my life, I sat on my living room couch a failure in wrestling and a failure in academics. **The man I had dreamed of becoming was not the man God desired me to be.**

IT IS JESUS

In my brokenness, I began to ask myself, "What am I missing?" and in the silence, I heard the answer: "It is Jesus." The words of John Paul II began to ring more and more true in my life, and they were the only consoling words I could find:

"It is Jesus, in fact, that you seek when you dream of happiness. He is waiting for you when nothing else you find satisfies you; he is the beauty to which you are so attracted; it is he who provokes you with that thirst for fullness that will not let you settle for compromise; it is he who urges you to shed the masks of a false life; it is he who reads in your hearts your most genuine choices, the choices that others try to stifle. It is Jesus who stirs in you the desire to do something great with your lives, the will to follow an ideal, the refusal to allow yourselves to be grounded down by mediocrity, the courage to commit yourselves humbly and patiently to improving yourselves and society, making the world more human and more fraternal."

All along, as I was dreaming of happiness and seeking to be satisfied by the things of this world, I was neglecting the one person who would truly make me happy, and truly satisfy. The entire time, I was basing my identity on the measure of success and failure without realizing I was losing my true identity in Christ.

In the next few weeks of my life, I spent hours each day in my bedroom praying and reflecting on life, realizing I placed all my happiness on things that were fading and things that were changing. The words of Saint Teresa of Avila became a reality in my life: "All things are passing; **God alone never changes.**" God, and God alone, never changes. At any point in our lives everything that we build can come crumbling down, and it is only God who is consistent and unchanging.

Late in my senior year of high school, I learned the most important lesson of my life: **There is no dream worth living for other than the dream of heaven.** And at that point in my life, I made the decision to start placing my hope, trust, and joy in God alone. I would no longer stake my identity on what I did, but rather on who I was as a child of God. I would no longer seek happiness in the fading things of this world, but in the beauty and splendor of a relationship with Jesus Christ.

Are you at the crossroads? Are you living for your own dreams of happiness? Are you seeking to be satisfied by the things of this world? Are you wearing the masks of a false life? If so, I ask you, do you know Jesus Christ? And I don't mean simply knowing about him or knowing what to say when religion teachers ask you questions. I am asking you whether or not you know that he loves you with an everlasting love, that he has been pursuing you your entire life, and that he desires more than anything to have a real and personal relationship with you.

I am so tired of talking to teenagers and adults and asking them, "What do you think you need to have a better relationship with God?" and hearing nothing more than empty answers. They always jump out with the answers "I need to pray more!" "I need to get to confession!" "I need Mass and adoration!" "I need to spend more time with my family and my youth group!" Yes, these are the *right* answers, but do you really believe them?

When you write down your priorities in life as God and family but then spend no time with God and no time with your family, you are lying to yourself. In high school I did an awakening activity in religion class. I had to write down all of my priorities and list them from 1 to 8. Then, throughout the next two weeks, I had to keep a calendar tracking where all my time went, and then rewrite my priorities as they related to my time. As it turned out, sports and TV were where God and family were supposed to be.

Jesus is everything. Having a relationship with him is more precious than anything this world has to offer. Greater than all the money in the world and all the success in the world is Jesus Christ. He is greater than your sports, your video games, your favorite band or TV show. He far surpasses your committees and clubs. And from the beginning of the world he has sought to have a relationship with you, because he sees you as more precious than anything else in this world too.

CALLED TO SANCTITY

"All Christians are called to holiness: 'Be perfect, as your heavenly Father is perfect.' In order to reach this perfection the faithful should use the strength dealt out to them by Christ's gift, so that . . . doing the Will of the Father in everything, they may wholeheartedly devote themselves to the glory of God and to the service of their neighbor. Thus the holiness of the People of God will grow in fruitful abundance, as is clearly shown in the history of the Church through the lives of so many saints." (Catechism of the Catholic Church, 2013)

At his first World Youth Day, after calling the youth of the world to a spiritual revolution of holiness, our Holy Father, Pope Benedict XVI, boldly proclaimed words that will rest with me until the day I die:

"The saints, as we said, are the true reformers. Now I want to express this in an even more radical way: **Only from the saints, only from God does true revolution come, the definitive**

way to change the world." (Vigil Mass, 2005)

What the world needs right now more than anything else is more saints. The world doesn't need another wrestler, or another Notre Dame student. The world doesn't need another American Idol or another movie star. The world doesn't need more pro athletes, or lawyers, or scientists, or engineers, or doctors, or politicians. The world doesn't need more priests and religious sisters, or more married men and women. **The world needs more saints!** We need *saintly* lawyers, scientists, and doctors; *saintly* athletes and musicians; *saintly* engineers and politicians; *saintly* priests and religious sisters; saintly husbands, wives, and children.

If we hope to bring about a complete and radical change to this world through holiness, then we need to fight with the holiness of the saints. The faithfulness and the apostolic witness of the saints is what changes the world. Within the Scriptures, the word used for "holy" and for "saint" is the same: *sanctus.* Over and over again, Saint Paul refers to the faithful Christians as the "holy ones" or the "saints." To be a faithful Christian is to be a part of the living communion of saints. To be a Christian means to die to yourself so that the holiness of Christ lives in you. "I have been crucified with Christ and I no longer live, but Christ lives in me. The life I live in the body, I live by faith in the Son of God, who loved me and gave himself for me." (Galatians 2:20) Thus, the Church boldly claims that "the way of perfection passes by way of the Cross. There is no holiness without renunciation and spiritual battle." (CCC, 2015)

Our revolution of holiness is a revolution of saints. If we wish to be holy, if we wish to bring change, we must live in imitation of the saints. We must live with apostolic credibility and apostolic witnessing. We must be radical like the saints. We must give everything like the saints. We must live wholeheartedly for the Kingdom of God and for the Gospel.

Pope Benedict XVI teaches this about the saints:

"Through these individuals, he wanted to show us how to be Christian: how to live life as it should be lived — according to God's way. The saints did not doggedly seek their own happiness, but simply wanted to give themselves, because the light of Christ had shone upon them. They show us the way to attain happiness; they show us how to be truly human. **Through all the ups and downs of history, they were the true reformers who constantly rescued it from plunging into the valley of darkness;** it was they who constantly shed upon it the light that was needed to make sense — even in the midst of suffering — of God's words spoken at the end of the work of creation: 'It is very good.'" (Vigil Mass, World Youth Day, 2005)

Pope Benedict spoke these words to the youth of the world, following his predecessor, John Paul II. Arguably more than any pope ever before him, Blessed John Paul the Great believed in the youth of the Church to change and renew the face of this world. He was the one who first spoke the Gospel to my heart and to the hearts of countless other young people. Before his death, in what turned out to be the last words he would ever write to the youth of the world, he proclaimed:

"Dear young people, the Church needs genuine witnesses for the new evangelization: men and women whose lives have been transformed by meeting with Jesus, men and women who are capable of communicating this experience to others. *The Church needs saints.* All are called to holiness, and holy people alone can renew humanity." (Message to the youth of the world on the occasion of the twentieth World Youth Day, August 6, 2004).

Heed the commission of the vicars of Christ! Listen to the words the Spirit of God speaks through the head of the Church and pray that the same Spirit will renew in you the gifts, the virtues, and the grace poured forth in the sacraments. **Become who you were born to be — become a saint!**

YOU HAVE WHAT IT TAKES

"Me, a saint? Ha! Yeah, right! What a joke!"

I remember back to my senior year in high school after I had given myself more fully over to Christ. I went on a retreat, and there God convicted my heart to change my sinful ways, especially in the realm of sexual impurity. I had spent much of my time in high school living in a number of impure relationships. Since I went to an all-guys' high school, I was able to date a number of girls at the same time without them knowing. I loved dating because I loved the thrill of the pursuit. Would the girl like me? How far would I be able to get her to go with me? I treated women like objects of my selfish game. I did not recognize their dignity and their true beauty. I used many women for my own pleasure, crossing way too many chastity lines. However, after this retreat, I came home and decided to change. I remember sitting down with some of my closest friends, people I cared about deeply, and telling them that I was going to change. I told them that I wasn't going to objectify women anymore and laugh at perverted jokes anymore. I remember them laughing at me, saying that I didn't have what it took to change, telling me that I would fail in my resolution of sexual purity within a few weeks.

I am not yet a saint, and I am not yet perfectly holy, but I have never given up my desire to be a saint and my pursuit of holiness. The reason for this is prayer. While some people in my life doubted my ability to change, in prayer I heard the quiet whisper of Jesus saying to me, **"You have what it takes!"** While others doubted, the Lord pushed. While others laughed, the Lord smiled at my efforts and my love for him. When I doubted myself, he gave me strength, reminding me that "nothing is impossible for God" (Luke 1:37) and that **"I can do all things through Christ who gives me strength."** (Philippians 4:13)

My dear brothers and sisters, I tell you this: *You have what it takes!* By right of your baptism and your confirmation, you have what it takes to be holy. You've got what it takes to be a saint. You've got what it takes to change this world not because of anything you do, but because of what God can and does do through you. **God made you amazing and can do amazing things through you.** The people of God carry with them the greatest power of all, the power of the Holy Spirit. The sacraments of baptism and confirmation literally grace you with every spiritual blessing you need to be holy. Do not allow people to crush your desire to be holy. Listen not to the voice of the evil one. He will speak through whomever he can to convince you that you are worthless and unable to build the Kingdom of God.

Beware of the greatest enemy in this respect: the voice in your head. I know that many of you hear a voice inside constantly saying you don't have what it takes, you are a failure, you are worthless. For some of you, these lies may have been planted in your mind by your peers, or your parents, or the undue pressure you place upon yourself. These lies may have been planted by the Devil, the master of lies. No matter where these lies came from, know that they are lies. *Never* allow yourself to buy into the lie that you don't have what it takes. **If you have been claimed as Christ's through the sacraments, then you have the power of the Holy Spirit within you and you can do anything.** To discredit yourself is to discredit God himself. Alone you can do nothing, but in Christ you can do everything! Remember, "I can do all things through Christ who gives me strength." (Philippians 4:13) "For nothing is impossible with God." (Luke 1:37)

Child of God, you have listened to far too many lies for far too long. Stop listening to the lies of Satan, and start listening to the voice of truth.

For those moments when the lies of Satan are pressing in hard, be ready to combat his lies with the voice of truth!

The Lies of the Devil	The Voice of Truth
You are a mistake.	You are my masterpiece. (Ephesians 2:10)
You are ugly.	You are fearfully and wonderfully made. (Psalm 139:14)
You are worthless.	For you were made in my image. (Genesis 1:27)
I hate my body.	Do you not know that your body is a temple of the Holy Spirit, who is in you, whom you have received from me? (1 Corinthians 6:19)
No one could ever love me. God could never love me.	I proved my love for you in that while you were still a sinner, I died for you! (Romans 5:8)
God doesn't want a sinner like me.	I came to seek and save what was lost. (Luke 19:10)
My life is falling apart.	I am before all things, and I hold all things together! (Colossians 1:17)
You are always anxious.	I bring peace. (Isaiah 9:6)
You are always depressed.	I bring joy. (Nehemiah 8:10)
You are always afraid.	I bring hope and courage. (Romans 5:1)
You'll amount to nothing.	You glorify me with your very existence. (Romans 11:36)
You can do nothing.	You can do anything when I give you strength. (Philippians 4:13)
You can't be great.	If you but have faith in me, you will not only do the works that I have done but greater ones than these. (John 14:12)
You aren't going to be taken care of.	I am your provider and I meet all your needs. (Matthew 6:31–33)
You're not enough!	If I am for you, who can be against you? (Romans 8:31)

You're not lovable and you will never be lovable.	I am love. (1 John 4:16) And I love you with an everlasting love. (Jeremiah 31:3/Malachi 1:2) "The Lord your God is in your midst, a mighty savior. He will rejoice over you with gladness and renew you in his love." (Zephaniah 3:17)
God's love isn't with you!	Nothing can separate you from my love. Neither death, nor life, nor demons, nor principalities, nor present things, nor future things, nor powers, nor height, nor depth, nor any other creature will be able to separate you from my everlasting love! (Romans 8:37–39).
I'm too busy for God and prayer.	"Seek first the Kingdom of God, and all these things will be given to you." (Matthew 6:33)
God doesn't hear me.	Ask and you shall receive. Knock and the door will be opened! (Matthew 7:8)
God is distant. He's not with me.	When you are brokenhearted, I am close to you. (Psalm 34:18)
God doesn't care about me.	I will never stop doing good to you. (Jeremiah 32:40) For you are my treasured possession. (Exodus 19:5)
God's not with me right now.	I am with you always and forever, even until the end of time. (Matthew 28:20)

PUT ASIDE THE RANGER

The Lord of the Rings: The Return of the King has an awesome scene that always inspires me. One of the main characters, Aragorn, is the rightful and true king of Gondor, a kingdom whose heart and soul rests on the strong leadership of its kings. For years, Gondor has had no king, and the people begin to lose hope that the reign of kings will ever be reestablished. Aragorn is the last hope to restore the kingship of Gondor, but one thing holds him back: His ancestor, King Elendil, won the ring of great power but fell prey to its evil, which corrupted him greatly. Aragorn fears that the power of being a king will lead to his own corruption, so instead of reclaiming the throne that is right-fully his, he lives in the shadows as a ranger.

The rangers are people of Middle Earth who are unnoticeable and calm even in the most dangerous situations. They are brave men, but they aren't noble men like the kings. Rangers are likened more to savages who live in the woods, while a king is a man who leads his kingdom in goodness and virtue. It was as if Aragorn did not believe that he had the leadership and the virtue to be a noble king, and so, living as a ranger, he hid himself in the shadows away from his true calling.

Aragorn finds himself in the midst of the greatest battle for Middle Earth the world has ever seen. Sauron, who represents the Devil, is launching an attack to destroy the entire human race, and his army is so large it is very likely that his siege will be successful and all humanity will be killed beneath the sword.

Aragorn seems to be losing hope just when Lord Elrond shows up. Elrond informs him that the army of men is so outnumbered that there is only one hope for mankind. Mankind needs a king to help restore hope, because they will only answer the call to fight from the true King of Gondor. Elrond pulls out from beneath his cloak the sword of the King of Gondor, the sword that once destroyed the army of Sauron, that could destroy Sauron once and for all. Elrond stares into Aragorn's eyes and says to him, "The man who can wield the power of this sword can summon to him an army more deadly than any that walks this earth. Put aside the ranger. Become who you were born to be." Aragorn takes the sword that represents his kingly status and marches to the Dimholt Road, the most deadly and threatening road, but the only road to victory. It is in Aragorn's reign as king that Gondor restores its might and glory and all of mankind is saved.

Why do I tell you this story? Why do I see this scene as so important to the Christian life? It is because to some degree, every one of us is just like Aragorn. Because of your baptism, you have everything it takes to be a great and glorious saint, a leader of goodness and virtue, and believe it or not, you have what it takes to share in the throne of Christ the King! Don't believe me? Then believe the Word of God:

> **Romans 8:16–18** "The Spirit himself testifies with our spirit that we are Gods children. Now if we are children, then we are heirs— heirs of God and co-heirs with Christ, if indeed we share in his sufferings in order that we may also share in his glory. I consider that our present sufferings are not worth comparing with the glory that will be revealed in us."

> **Galatians 4:7** "So you are no longer a slave, but a son; and since you are a son, God has made you also an heir."

> **Titus 3:7** "Having been justified by his grace, we might become heirs having the hope of eternal life."

Do you see where I am going with this? In the waters of baptism, we became the adopted sons and daughters of God, and as sons and daughters, we are co-heirs with Christ, sharing the throne of Christ the King. Simply put, **we were born for the sake of heaven.** Our purpose here on earth is to know, love, and serve God in this life and to be happy with him in the next. We were born to live as saints, and to spend all of eternity as saints in heaven with Jesus Christ. But like Aragorn, we are afraid of this throne; we are afraid to live the life of the person we were born to be.

Aragorn was afraid to live the life he was born to live, and so instead he hid from it. As a ranger, he hid in the shadows, going unnoticed by men. How often do we do this? How often do we as Christians hide our faith in the shadows, afraid of what people will think of us, afraid of being judged or not being accepted, or afraid of letting God down, letting others down, or being let down ourselves?

War is at hand. The army of the Devil is strong and rises up against us Christians, and yes, we are outnumbered. We are outnumbered in our schools and our workplaces. The Devil has an army of sin that looks like it is impossible to destroy, but we have the holiness of the saints, the sword of the Spirit, and the promise of victory in Jesus Christ.

The Holiness Revolution, the revolution of the saints, has begun. The question is, will you fight with us? Remember, you have two options: Either you will live to change this world, or the world will change you.

"Put aside the ranger. Become who you were born to be."

TALK ABOUT IT.

(If reading with a group, use these questions for discussion.)

1. What was your reaction to the statistics at the beginning of this chapter? Did they shock you?

2. When you read statistics like this, how do you react? Do you act like they don't matter? Or does it change your actions?

3. Do you seek happiness in Jesus or do you seek happiness in the things of this world?

4. What is the answer to the worlds hurt and pain? How can we possibly be the solution? Is there hope? Why?

5. If Jesus is the answer to the hurt and pain in this world, then how should that impact our life? What are we doing about it?

6. Do you see living a saintly life as "rebellious?" Why or why not?

7. Why are you doing to bring the Kingdom of God to earth?

8. How often do you say I'm bored? What could you do when you are bored to make a difference in the world?

9. Do you believe that you have what it takes to be a saint? Why or why not?

10. What lies of the Devil have you bought into? What do you think the voice of truth would say to you?

11. Do you, like Aragorn, hide from the calling you have received? How?

TAKE ACTION

ACTION STEP 1: Choose now what two things you will do next time you think to yourself "I'm bored." Then, do it.

ACTION STEP 2: Write a list of your top five priorities. Then, write down next to your list how many hours you spend with each thing. Looking at the time you spend with each priority, do your top priorities get the most time?

ACTION STEP 3: Write down all the lies that you have convinced yourself of. After finishing the list, find a safe place to burn them (your bedroom trashcan is not a safe place). Forget about these lies and let the voice of truth speak to you.

ACTION STEP 4: Talk to someone you know that has been listening to the loves of the Devil and share with them the Scripture verses from above.

ACTION STEP 5: Aragorn had a calling from the Lord that he hid from. Write down what you think the Lord is calling you to and tape it to your bedroom wall in a place that you will see every day so that you can't hide from that calling.

www.Holiness Revolution.com

3

THE REBEL JESUS

Before we can go any further, we must turn and look at our king. We can never fight in this revolution of holiness if we do not know the king for whom and in whom we fight. We can never be a saint without having a deep love and loyalty to Christ the King. After all, any holiness we obtain is merely the holiness of God alive in us, and any change we bring about is simply his spirit of renewal working through us.

One evening when I was in college I was gathered with about five hundred other students at a Christian conference in Michigan. The conference came to a climax as we all convened in a tight gathering space to pray for the conversion of the world. Five hundred college Christians, crammed in a room fit for far fewer than what we had, prayed for three hours straight for the conversion of the world. We prayed for the end of abortion and poverty, for the end of war and hatred, for the spread of the Gospel and for the conversion of pagan lands. We prayed against the tactics of the Devil and the sins of this world. We were aggressive, and we were united as the body of Christ. v

Inspired by this, I was praying intensely and begging the Lord Jesus to help me change the world for his glory. For the first time ever, my eyes were truly open to see just how badly the world needed conversion and renewal. Everywhere I looked I saw pain, hurt, and darkness. I wanted to be the light of Christ for the world, but I was struggling so hard to do it. I was fighting and fighting, but continually falling prey to the same petty sins. I would be given opportunities to minister to others and out of fear I would, like a coward, shy away from those opportunities. In my prayer that evening, I saw an image. I was a warrior in the army of the Lord and I had just returned home from battle. I journeyed up a high set of stairs laid with gold and protected by fellow warriors. After reaching the last stair, I came up to a massive doorway, and as I stood before the doors, they opened by themselves. Upon entering, I saw a throne in the distance. I hastened down the column-lined hall and quickly found myself face-to-face with Jesus Christ, my sovereign king, seated upon his throne. I fell to my knees weeping before that glorious throne.

And then, I heard his voice. "My servant, why do you weep?" I could not answer, but he knew why I was there. My armor was destroyed. My face was blackened with dirt and my hands were bloodied from battle. I had been fighting, but I had been losing. It seemed like the harder I fought, the harder I fell. Not needing an answer to his question, my king arose, took off his armor, and handed it to me, saying, "Fight with this, my son." And then, holding his armor, more radiant than all the stars of the sky, I understood what it meant to be a servant of God.

For so long, I had fought with my own strength and my own power. Time after time I waged war against the world, the flesh, and the Devil, and time after time I fell short of glory. God's warrior fights not with his own strength, but with the strength of his king. If you fight with your own strength, then you fight for yourself. If you fight with his strength, then you fight for his kingdom. The king we serve is one who gives us his armor. **He gives his very self to us.** He is a generous king who not only leads us into battle, but fights through us in battle.

The more I pray, the more I learn of the one I serve. The more I learn of him, the more I am amazed and humbled by his great love. Jesus Christ is truly the king of kings and the lord of lords. If you wish to know more of the glory of this king, you must pray. **Only in prayer will you meet him face-to-face. Only in prayer will he be revealed to your heart.** If you approach him in prayer, you will learn that he is the most incredible king we could ever imagine. Truly he is so amazing and so phenomenal that words would only fail in describing his glory. Though the glory of God is indescribable, I believe that one preacher, Dr. S. M. Lockridge, came very close, in his famous sermon called the "Seven Way King." In this sermon, he strives to sum up the glory of Christ the King:

"The Bible says my King is the King of the Jews. He's the King of Israel. He's the King of righteousness. He's the King of the ages. He's the King of Heaven. He's the King of glory. He's the King of kings, and He's the Lord of lords. That's my King. I wonder, do you know Him?

"My King is a sovereign King. No means of measure can define His limitless love. He's enduringly strong. He's entirely sincere. He's eternally steadfast. He's immortally graceful. He's imperially powerful. He's impartially merciful. Do you know Him?

"He's the greatest phenomenon that has ever crossed the horizon of this world. He's God's Son. He's the sinner's Savior. He's the peak of civilization. He's unparalleled. He's unprecedented. He is the loftiest idea in literature. He's the highest personality in philosophy. He's the fundamental doctrine of true theology. He's the only one qualified to be an all-sufficient Savior. I wonder if you know Him today?

"He supplies strength for the weak. He's available for the tempted and the tried. He sympathizes and He saves. He strengthens and sustains. He guards and He guides. He heals the sick. He cleanses the lepers. He forgives sinners. He discharges debtors. He delivers the captives. He defends the feeble. He blesses the young. He serves the unfortunate. He regards the aged. He rewards the diligent, and He beautifies the meager. I wonder if you know Him?

"He's the key to knowledge. He's the wellspring of wisdom. He's the doorway of deliverance. He's the pathway of peace. He's the roadway of righteousness. He's the highway of holiness. He's the gateway of glory. Do you know Him?

"His light is matchless. His goodness is limitless. His mercy is everlasting. His love never changes. His word is enough. His grace is sufficient. His reign is righteous, and His yoke is easy and His burden is light. I wish I could describe Him to you. Yes, He's indescribable. He's incomprehensible. He's invincible. He's irresistible. You can't get Him out of your mind. You can't get Him out of your head. You can't outlive Him, and you can't live without Him.

"The Pharisees couldn't stand Him but they found out they couldn't stop Him. Pilate couldn't find any fault in Him. Herod couldn't kill Him. Death couldn't handle Him, and the grave couldn't hold Him. I wonder if you know Him? That's my King!"

These words are so beautifully and powerfully spoken, yet they still can't contain his glory. Imagine for one moment the glory of the throne of Christ the King. Imagine for one minute just how magnificent his great and glorious throne must be. Saint John shares with us his vision of the throne of Christ the King in the book of Revelation:

"A throne was there in heaven, and on the throne sat one whose appearance sparkled like jasper and carnelian. Around the throne was a halo as brilliant as an emerald. Surrounding the throne I saw twenty-four other thrones on which twenty-four elders sat, dressed in white garments and with gold crowns on their heads. From the throne came flashes of lightning, rumblings, and peals of thunder. Seven flaming torches burned in front of the throne, which are the seven spirits of God. In front of the throne was something that resembled a sea of glass like crystal. In the center and around the throne, there were four living creatures covered with eyes in front and in back. The first creature resembled a lion, the second was like a calf, the third had a face like that of a human being, and the fourth looked like an eagle in flight. The four living creatures, each of them with six wings, were covered with eyes inside and out. Day and night they do not stop exclaiming: **'Holy, holy, holy is the Lord God almighty, who was, and who is, and who is to come.'** Whenever the living creatures give glory and honor and thanks to the one who sits on the throne, who lives forever and ever, the twenty-four elders fall down before the one who sits on the throne and worship Him, who lives forever and ever. They throw down their crowns before the throne, exclaiming 'Worthy are you, Lord our God, to receive glory and honor and power, for you created all things!'" (Revelation 4:1–11)

Dang, now that's a throne! That's how a king should live! Imagine the glory of this scene, with twenty-four surrounding thrones and flashes of lightning, peals of thunder, flames of torches, the blaring of trumpets, and the songs of praise. This is the glory of our king and of his glorious throne.

As I did that one night in college, and as Saint John does in the book of Revelation, find yourself in prayer before the throne of Christ the King and see what happens. Hebrews 4:15–16 calls us to approach the throne of Christ, and to do so with confidence. "For we do not have a high priest who is unable to sympathize with our weaknesses, but we have one who has been tested in every way that we are—yet without sin. Let us then confidently approach the throne of grace, so that we may receive mercy and find grace to help us in our time of need."

Servant of God, if you wish to fight beside our Lord in this revolution of holiness, you need his mercy, his grace, and his armor. He is waiting for you to come to him as a beggar, and to plead for mercy, for grace, and for any help that you need to serve him better. If you are fighting with your own strength, there is strength greater than your own to be had. If you are tired and burnt out, there is zeal and passion greater than your own to be had. If you are fearful or doubtful, there is fortitude and confidence greater than your own to be had. There is grace to be had, my fellow warrior. **You can fight with the strength of Christ the King — and in him, we can have victory.**

What areas of your life have you not yet surrendered? In what areas are you trying to overcome your weaknesses on your own? Where do you need strength? Where do you need courage? Are you fighting with your own armor? Are you fighting at all? Are you glorifying yourself with your strengths? Come, my brothers and sisters, and let us confidently approach the throne of grace:

Lord, grant to me what I need the most. Heal me where I need healing the most. Where I fight with my own strength, let me fight with yours. Where I am weakest, let me be strongest. Where I am insecure, let me be confident. Give me the grace to fight with you, to fight for you, and to fight in you. You, Lord, are my king, and there is no other.

BEWARE OF THE FALSE IDOL!

One of the most shocking moments of my life was when I realized I was worshipping a false image of Jesus Christ. I called myself Christian and went to Mass on Sundays, assuming that I knew who Jesus was, but sadly, the image of Jesus that had been presented to me didn't size up much with the true image of Christ that I encountered later in my life. I wonder if the image of Jesus you have been presented with is a Jesus worth following? **When you think of Jesus, are you floored? Are you amazed like the early disciples?** Is he the kind of guy you would drop everything for and follow? Probably not.

That is the reason we claim to be followers of Christ, but drop nothing. The early disciples encountered the real and living Christ and in doing so, they dropped everything they had and followed him. They did not go on living their former way of life. Think about Andrew and Peter, James and John. When Jesus approached these men on the Sea of Galilee he said one simple thing: "Follow me and I will make you fishers of men." Scripture says that these four men *immediately* dropped their nets and followed him. They left their jobs, their families, their security, their comfort zones, their dreams, their wants, and their desires — they dropped everything and followed him.

The reason the early disciples dropped everything immediately was because when they encountered the living God, they encountered someone worth dropping everything for. There was something different about this man, something *worth* following. The reason most of us haven't dropped everything and followed Jesus is because many of us have spent our entire lives worshipping a false image of Jesus Christ. I grew up in a faithful home and went to Catholic schools from the time I was four years old, but as a child, the faith always seemed wimpy. For me, religion was associated with emotional warmth, not mission. As a child, I was bombarded with lollipops and rainbow stickers that read "Jesus loves you" or "Jesus is a cool dude." **Jesus was portrayed as a Claymation cartoon skipping through the magical land of sugarplums and daydreams distributing cotton candy and bubble gum to the children who gathered at his feet.** I learned that Jesus was a person who teaches us to be nice and to share our toys with our friends. As I grew up, the misconceptions continued. It seemed like the only doctrines I ever learned were that God wants people to be good, tolerant, and fair to each other and that the central goal of life is to be happy and to feel good about oneself. God was needed in one's life only when there were problems to be fixed. There was no notion of simply loving God for the sake of loving God, staying steadfast in prayer, repenting from sin, or encouraging others to live the Gospel. There definitely wasn't the notion of being a servant of God, or fighting in a revolution of holiness — after all, the word *revolution* sounds violent, and we Christians are supposed to be nice. It seemed as though instead of my being called to be a servant of God, God was meant to be my servant, helping me when I needed to turn to him.

Jesus was not viewed as someone who placed demands on my life. Rather, he was seen as the ultimate nice guy who teaches us how to be nice to others. I thought that the only thing Jesus wanted was for us to be happy and secure, to be tolerant of all people and love all people.

Ultimately, my idea of Christ was that of a happy, smiley man who went around telling us to be nice to people. While of course Jesus calls us to love others, he does more than tell us to be nice. **Nice people of-**

ten are too afraid to defend truth. Nice people are afraid to evangelize. Nice people are too afraid to stick up when injustice is being done. Jesus calls us to love, but love is not always *nice.*

People also seemed to be obsessed with telling me that Jesus was my buddy. It seemed I was constantly told that the relationship I should have with Jesus was one in which Jesus was my friend and that I should talk to him just like I talked to my friends. While this has an element of truth to it, it can also cause a lot of harm if misunderstood. The problem with treating Jesus like my buddy is that if I disagree with my buddies, I ignore them. Thus, for many years of high school, when I disagreed with Jesus's teachings in the Bible or in the Church, I would just ignore them. This led me to sin, disobedience, and unhappiness. Ultimately, Jesus can't be just like one of our friends, because if we disagree with Jesus, we are called to obedience. Jesus is more than just a friend; he is our king. This king calls us to live a certain way of life and to do certain things for his kingdom.

Growing up, I came into contact with many different images of Jesus, but it seemed that there had been a missing image. My childhood church had white walls with no statues. Instead of a crucifix hanging front and center, there hung a large image of the risen Lord on the cross, which I call a "ressurectifix." While we should rejoice in the Resurrection, at the heart of the Mass and at the heart of our Christian life is the suffering and death of Jesus Christ; but in my church, there was no crucifix to be found. The image of Christ that was missing from my childhood was that of the crucified Lord.

Jesus crucified on the cross, completely covered with blood and dirt, is the most real image of Jesus Christ we can find. Jesus was a man who was arrested and killed for treason, for claiming to be a king. Jesus was a rebel, an all-out revolutionary; he was the leader of a movement against the world's standards. He confronted people for the injustices of his time;

he broke the Jewish laws, for which he could be killed; he turned tables over and yelled at people when they disrespected his Father; and most of all, he chastised the Pharisees, saying over and over again, "Woe to you!" which essentially means "Go to hell!"

Jesus wasn't always "nice." It wasn't very nice of him to tell the Pharisees that if they didn't change their ways then they would go to hell — but it was loving. It wasn't very nice of him to knock tables over in the temple — but it was loving. The most real image of Jesus we can be presented with is that of him on the cross.

If you want to know who the man Jesus Christ was, stop listening to the hippies pushing their own agenda and molding Jesus into some flower-power, love-train engineer. Recognize that when we as Christians profess, "God is love," we mean that Jesus Christ demonstrates, proves, and teaches us what love is while he suffers the most painful and humiliating death imaginable to man. Love is an unconditional gift of yourself.

THIS IS LOVE

"This is love: not that we loved God, but that he loved us and sent his Son as an atoning sacrifice for our sins." (1 John 4:10)

Ponder with me for one moment the Incarnation. Truly this is the world's most astonishing event. God, who has no beginning or end, became a mortal man, with a beginning and an end. The Creator of the world stepped into the world. The Creator became a creature. The artist became the art. He who is God, he who lacks nothing and is everything, the alpha and omega, the king of kings and lord of lords, the all-powerful and the all-knowing, he became a little baby boy. What great love this is that God humbled himself to become man, and not only man, but child. In Jesus, we have the perfect witness of humility and the perfect witness of love.

Catholic writer, Peter Kreeft, puts it like this: "The gospel is a love story — the story of God's love for man. And the story of the world's conversion is also a love story — the story of man's love for this God. . . . It is a story of crazy, passionate love that led the eternal Creator, infinitely perfect and lacking nothing, to become a mortal man and suffer torture, death, and hell to save us rebels from our sins. We sinned for no reason but lack of love, and He redeemed us for no reason but excess of love. . . . Only the hard or despairing heart can look on that face on the Cross, know who that is, what He is doing, what love made Him do it, and whose sin made it necessary, without melting." *Kreeft, Peter J. "Jesus Christ." Catholic Christianity. San Francisco: Ignatius Press, 2001. 69, 70, 72.*

God becomes man for our sake because we were sinners who needed redemption. And Jesus, God who is man, displays the greatest act of love for us in that while we were still sinners, he died for us (Romans 5:8). Jesus's love for us has no bounds. He was willing to suffer the most painful and agonizing death simply because he loved us. We have all heard the Gospel, but the Gospel clothed in the false image of Christ can't fully penetrate our hearts. At the heart of the Gospel, at the heart of the person of Jesus Christ, is the crucifix.

This is the Good News of the Gospel: Jesus Christ, the eternal Son of God, became man, suffered, and died for you. At the moment he was on the cross, he foresaw all of your sins and all of the ways you would reject him, and out of complete love, **he died uniquely for you.** If you were the only person in the world he would have still died for you, because you matter that much to him. If you're looking for true love, if you're looking for true acceptance — it's been in front of you all this time. "Fear not, for I have redeemed you; I have called you by name and you are mine." (Isaiah 43:2)

You see, the truest image of love is not a valentine heart or a naked midget in a diaper holding a bow and arrow; it's not a ten-year-old girl's weird obsession with boy-band members; it's not a relationship status on Facebook or a four-hour phone conversation. The truest image of love is nothing other than a bloody crucifix: God, lacking nothing and bearing no fault of his own, pouring his blood out on the cross for love of sinners. My beautiful wife and I truly believe that if we are to ever love each other, it doesn't mean that we will have wonderful fuzzy feelings for one another at all times, but it does mean that even when we don't want to serve each other, we will lay our lives down in service like Christ did on the cross. This true meaning of love was so important to my wife and me that on our wedding day, we adopted the Croatian tradition of exchanging vows while holding a crucifix, reminding ourselves that our human love is meant to model Christ's divine, self-giving love.

While Jesus hung on the cross suffering for our sake, he taught the world a very powerful lesson about what love is. Often, people define love as an emotion or an uncontrollable desire, but Jesus shows us love is an action. Ultimately, love is the action of giving a sincere gift of yourself to another. Jesus did not give us a present to show us he loved us; he gave us himself. One of the greatest lessons we can learn from Jesus is that **love is a sincere and true gift of self.** But Jesus didn't just give himself to us on the cross; he went even further. Jesus gives himself to all humanity throughout all of history with the incredible gift of the Eucharist. The most amazing thing about the Holy Mass is that at Mass, love himself comes to us and we receive love himself into our bodies. We become one with love.

"For I am convinced that neither death nor life, neither angels nor demons, neither the present nor the future, nor any powers, neither height nor depth, nor anything else in all creation, will be able to separate us from the love of God that is in Christ Jesus our Lord." (Romans 8:38–39) This is the power of the love of Jesus Christ This is the power of our king's great love

Now that we know this great revelation of God's love for us, we must act on it. God's love is a call to action. We have to respond to the love of God with love for him and with love for one another. "Since God so loved us, we also ought to love one another." (1 John 4:11) We are called to love the world with the same self-sacrificial, self-giving love of Jesus

Christ. In a world of selfishness, we are called to be a gift. In a world of egotism, we are called to serve the other. In a world that cares only about what's in it for me, we are called to "humbly regard others as more important than ourselves." (Philippians 2:3) Don't take the love of God for granted. **Respond.**

JESUS THE MODEL REVOLUTIONARY

The real image of Christ is that of a man worth living for. Jesus is a man worth following. When you think of Jesus, you should be floored and amazed like the early disciples. He should be the kind of guy you drop everything for and follow. The early disciples encountered the real and living Christ and dropped everything. They did not go on living their former way of life, and neither should we.

Let's stop living like the fake Jesus and start living like the real Jesus. The real Jesus was more than just a nice guy — he was a rebel! He knew when to be gentle and when to be bold. He knew when to be humble and when to confront others. He was compassionate and loving, but not overemotional. He was not held down by fear, but was bold and courageous.

Jesus was a man of virtue. Are we?

Jesus was a man of action. Are we?

Jesus cared for the dignity of every human life. Do we?

Jesus stuck up for the poor and the outcasts of society. Do we?

Jesus laid his life down serving others. Do we?

His love for you cost him his life. What has your love for him cost you?

Jesus Christ died to teach us how to live. We so often think the only reason Christ died was to grant us eternal life, and while this is true, I think he died for more than this. He died to teach us how to live this life. We don't have to wait for heaven to begin living our eternal life, because the fullness of life can be ours here and now. "I have come so that you might have life, and have it to the fullest." (John 10:10)

We need to be mindful that the life of Christ, and the life he calls us to live, is downright, absolutely crazy! Over and over again Jesus uses paradoxes that would make most people think Christians are completely insane. This is the crazy life of a Christian:

The rich are poor. The poor are rich.

The first shall be last. The last shall be first.

The exalted are humbled. The humble are exalted.

The one who would be greatest among us must be servant of all.

The one who loves his life will lose it, while he who hates his life will live forever.

The one who gives receives. The one who forgives is forgiven.

The one who mourns rejoices. The one who is weak is strong.

Give preference to one another in showing honor.

Regard others as more important than yourself.

If you wish to be filled, empty yourself.

If you hope to win, surrender.

If you are to be greatest, be least.

Rejoice when you're persecuted. Glory in tribulation.

Bless those who curse you. Love the man who hates you.

Do good to those who harm you.

If you wish to live, you must die to yourself.

Erasmus wrote in his work *Praise of Folly*, "The biggest fools of all appear to be those who have once been wholly possessed by zeal for

Christian piety. They squander their possessions, ignore insults, submit to being cheated, make no distinction between friends and enemies, shun pleasure, sustain themselves on fasting, vigils, tears, toil and humiliations, scorn life and desire only death. . . . What else can that be but madness?"

Christianity is the greatest stupidity this world has ever seen, but it is the smartest stupidity we could ever live. *Truly Christianity is the only kind of life worth living, because* **it's the only life in which you live for something greater than yourself.** Yes, there is great pain and sacrifice involved in following Christ's example, but there are even greater rewards. And if we choose not to follow his example, there is even greater pain.

FOLLOW HIM

Jesus was not a wimpy man who walked around asking people to be nice and follow him. People followed Christ because he was worth following. Jesus Christ was a revolutionary. In fact, the Bible tells us the first Christians were thought of as revolutionaries. Throughout the Acts of the Apostles, the disciples of Jesus are described as being people "who have been creating a disturbance all over the world." (17:6) Let's follow in Jesus's footsteps. Let's follow in the footsteps of the early disciples. **Let's start causing a disturbance all over the world for the glory of God.** This is what revolutionaries do They turn the world upside down. They bring about a complete and radical change. **They make things happen!**

Following Jesus in a world that has rejected him is the most rebellious thing you could ever do. The real rebels are those who fall in love with Jesus Christ. The real rebels are those who do the will of God. The real rebels are those who are bold enough to live their faith. **The real rebels are those who are brave enough to dare to be saints!**

But I warn you, being a Christian isn't easy. Doing the virtuous thing all the time isn't easy. Admitting your sin and changing your life isn't easy. Loving your enemies and sticking up for the rejected isn't easy. Standing up to the injustices of the world isn't easy. Giving hurts, and sometimes it hurts badly. But I promise you, **it is worth it.** It is worth all the pain and suffering and hardship in the world to follow the greatest king who has ever set foot in this world. It's worth dropping what is important to you to be a better follower of the man we know is God.

Jesus is worth your time.

He is worth your energy and your enthusiasm.

Jesus is worth your life.

Our whole lives we've been told by our parents and our teachers to be "safe." But Jesus says, **"Quit being safe!** Get out of the boat and walk on water. Go through the narrow gate. Put out into deep waters. **Do something that isn't easy, or comfortable, or safe.** Come, follow me!"

TALK ABOUT IT.

(If reading with a group, use these questions for discussion.)

1. Are you fighting with your own armor? Where do you need strength and grace to fight better?

2. Jesus teaches us that love is a gift of self. What has love been in your mind up until this point? With this new understanding, would you consider yourself a 'loving' person?

3. Is the Jesus you've been presented with growing up, a man worth following? Is he worth dropping everything for?

4. If he is, then why haven't your dropped everything? What's holding you back?

5. Really think about this:

   a. Jesus was a man of virtue. Are you?

   b. Jesus was a man of action. Are you?

   c. Jesus cared for the dignity of every human life. Do you?

   d. Jesus stuck up for the poor and the outcasts of society. Do you?

   e. Jesus laid his life down serving others. Do you?

6. Jesus's love for you cost him his life. What has your love for him cost you?

7. In the Acts of the Apostles, the disciples of Jesus are described as being people "who have been creating a disturbance all over the world." (17:6) What kind of disturbance are you being called to create for Jesus?

8. If you decide today to give Jesus your life, what needs to change?

TAKE ACTION

ACTION STEP 1: Start praying a morning consecration to Jesus:

Lord Jesus Christ,
today I choose to live for you.
Today I choose to live for something greater than myself.
Today I choose to be on mission.
I will follow you no matter where you lead me,
I will love those you place before me.
I will seek out the lost, the lonely, the rejected, the forgotten.
I will love until it hurts.
Make me more like you Jesus.
It is no longer I who lives, but You who lives in me.

Amen.

ACTION STEP 2: Love is a sincere gift of self. Choose three ways that you are going to give yourself to another person through a loving act. Carry this action on. Don't just do it once and stop!

- Serve your parents or siblings without them asking.
- Listen to someone who needs someone to listen to them.
- Compliment people and build them up with uplifting words.
- Give up your preference for the sake of someone else's preference.

ACTION STEP 3: Do something uncomfortable for Jesus.

- Hang out with someone you typically wouldn't hang out with.
- Tell someone that they are loved by Jesus.
- Do something to make yourself last.
- Call a friend out on their sinfulness in a loving way.

www.Holiness†Revolution.com

PART TWO:

THE
REVOLUTION OF
YOUR HEART

4

STRIVING FOR HOLINESS

So you want to be a revolutionary? You want to join this great revolution of holiness and bring about a complete and radical change in this world? Well then I have news for you: **The revolution starts with you!**

The first aspect of this world that needs a complete and radical change is your own heart. *__You need to change before you can ever change this world.__* The Holiness Revolution must first start in your own heart. Then, and only then, can you help to change this depraved and corrupt generation.

Did you know that when you were baptized, you were baptized into a spiritual battle? From the moment your soul was claimed by Christ and you received the everlasting mark of a Christian, you have been hunted down by none other than an army of demons seeking to "steal, slaughter, and destroy." (John 10:10) We were born into a battle against sin and Satan, but in baptism "we know that our old self was crucified with him so that our sinful body might be done away with, that we might no longer be in slavery to sin." (Romans 6:6)

You, Christians, you must strive ardently to break free from the yoke of slavery to sin and be born again as God's holy ones, as the saints. Do you want to see revival? Do you want to see renewal? Do you want revolution? Then strive for the holiness you are called to live.

FREEDOM IS AT HAND

For it is in Jesus Christ that we find true and everlasting freedom. Jesus sets us free from slavery to sin and death. "For you know that it was not with perishable things such as silver or gold that you were redeemed from the empty way of life . . . but with the precious blood of Christ, a lamb without blemish or defect." (1 Peter 1:18–19) We have all fallen prey to the chains of sin that hold us in bondage, but **we need not remain slaves.**

If you wish to be a revolutionary, if you wish to be a saint, "sin must not reign over your mortal bodies so that you obey your desires. And do not present the parts of your bodies to sin as weapons for wickedness, but present yourselves to God as . . . weapons for righteousness. **For sin is not to have any power over you."** (Romans 6:13–14)

So what will it be? Will you be a weapon for wickedness or a weapon for righteousness? If you hope to be a weapon for righteousness, then you need to turn away from your former way of life and live wholly for the Gospel. Let not your mortal flesh reign over you any longer. Be free from your sin. Be free from worldliness. **Be free to love without limits.**

BECOME A WEAPON OF RIGHTEOUSNESS

What does it mean to be a weapon of righteousness? Who are these "weapons" for the Lord? Pope Benedict answers this for us when he says, "The saints, as we said, are the true reformers . . . only from the saints, only from God does true revolution come, the definitive way to change the world." (Vigil Mass, WYD, 2005) The true weapons of righteousness are the saints, those who are true disciples of Jesus Christ, those who actually strive for sanctity day after day.

Living like a saint is pretty simple. The saints are true disciples of Jesus, and most of us should already know what it means to be a true disciple of Jesus Christ. The problem isn't in the knowing; it's in the doing. Discipleship, holiness, sanctity — it's all simple, but it's not at all easy. It's simple because to be a saint means to do everything God asks you to do; it is easy to know what God asks of us because he has given us the Scriptures and the Church to communicate his word to us. But if it were as easy as it were simple, we would have a world of saints instead of a world of sinners.

I beg of you, read carefully the words in this chapter. Do not skim over them quickly, but instead, examine them. Examine your heart. Examine your way of life. **I hope to challenge you in this chapter in a way you have never been challenged.** I'm not selling you an easy version of Christianity, because Jesus didn't call us to that; rather, I want to unveil the words of Scripture so that you might read them in a way that you have never read them before. Be patient. Read slowly. Think. Pray. Discern.

Saint Paul tells us in the letter to the Philippians to "work out your salvation with fear and trembling." (Philippians 2:12) Might I be so bold as to suggest that the vast majority of American Catholics, and the vast majority of the American Christian people, have completely ignored this exhortation of Saint Paul? Instead of working out our salvation with fear and trembling, many of us have fallen prey to falsely assuming that we are guaranteed a place in heaven.

Yes, I'm speaking about the Catholics who only go to church on Christmas and Easter, but I'm also speaking to the Catholics in the pews each week; I'm speaking of the Catholics who don't do any service work and those who are involved in all kinds of activities and parish life. Chances are, I'm speaking about you and about myself. I would even include the vast majority of American priests and religious in this category as well — goodintentioned people who have given a lot to Christ, but who assume they are going to heaven instead of living a life that works out salvation with fear and trembling. Be honest with yourself: Up until this point in your life, have you lived in such a way that you assumed you would go to heaven because you are basically a good person?

Why should we work out our salvation with fear and trembling? Because **the demands of Christ Jesus are far greater than the demands we place on ourselves.** The demands of Christ Jesus are far greater than the Sunday obligation and a prayer offered here and there.

Slowly read these words from the Gospel of Matthew. As you do so, hear the words of Jesus telling you and me what it means to be a disciple, what it means to be a weapon for righteousness, and determine whether or not you are truly living the life that Jesus Christ has asked you to live as his disciple.

Matthew 6:19–21, 24: Treasures in Heaven

"Do not store up for yourselves treasures on earth, where moths and vermin destroy, and where thieves break in and steal. But store up for yourselves treasures in heaven, where moths and vermin do not destroy, and where thieves do not break in and steal. For where your treasure is, there your heart will be also.

"No one can serve two masters. Either you will hate the one and love the other, or you will be devoted to the one and despise the other. You cannot serve both God and money."

Matthew 6:25–34: Do Not Worry

"Therefore I tell you, do not worry about your life, what you will eat or drink; or about your body, what you will wear. Is not life more than food, and the body more than clothes? Look at the birds of the air; they do not sow or reap or store away in barns, and yet your heavenly Father feeds them. Are you not much more valuable than they? Can any one of you by worrying add a single hour to your life?

"And why do you worry about clothes? See how the flowers of the field grow. They do not labor or spin. Yet I tell you that not even Solomon in all his splendor was dressed like one of these. If that is how God clothes the grass of the field, which is here today and tomorrow is thrown into the fire, will he not much more clothe you—you of little faith? So do not worry, saying, 'What shall we eat?' or 'What shall we drink?' or 'What shall we wear?' For the pagans run after all these things, and your heavenly Father knows that you need them. But seek first his kingdom and his righteousness, and all these things will be given to you as well. Therefore do not worry about tomorrow, for tomorrow will worry about itself. Each day has enough trouble of its own."

Matthew 7:13–14: The Narrow and Wide Gates

"Enter through the narrow gate. For wide is the gate and broad is the road that leads to destruction, and many enter through it. But small is the gate and narrow the road that leads to life, and only a few find it."

Matthew 7:15–20: True and False Prophets

"Watch out for false prophets. They come to you in sheep's clothing, but inwardly they are ferocious wolves. By their fruit you will recognize them. Do people pick grapes from thornbushes, or figs from thistles? Likewise, every good tree bears good fruit, but a bad tree bears bad fruit. A good tree cannot bear bad fruit, and a bad tree cannot bear good fruit. Every tree that does not bear good fruit is cut down and thrown into the fire. Thus, by their fruit you will recognize them."

Matthew 7:21–23: True and False Disciples

"Not everyone who says to me, 'Lord, Lord,' will enter the kingdom of heaven, but only the one who does the will of my Father who is in heaven. Many will say to me on that day, 'Lord, Lord, did we not prophesy in your name and in your name drive out demons and in your name perform many miracles?' Then I will tell them plainly, 'I never knew you. Away from me, you evildoers!'"

Matthew 7:24–27: The Wise and Foolish Builders

"Therefore everyone who hears these words of mine and puts them into practice is like a wise man who built his house on the rock. The rain came down, the streams rose, and the winds blew and beat against that house; yet it did not fall, because it had its foundation on the rock. But everyone who hears these words of mine and does not put them into practice is like a foolish man who built his house on sand. The rain came down, the streams rose, and the winds blew and beat against that house, and it fell with a great crash."

THE NARROW PATH

Day after day, night after night, my heart burns for the salvation of souls. The words of Jesus Christ on the cross, "I thirst" (John 19:28), have begun to ring so true in my life as I have countless times prayed the Chaplet of Divine Mercy in tears, begging Christ Jesus to bring all sinners to himself, of which I am the foremost. I have not written this book because I think the notion of a revolution of holiness is cool and trendy and could sell. I have written this book because I thirst for your soul and all souls. I truly believe that our world needs an intense renewal. I fear that if the world continues living as though God and his law are not relevant, then many souls may see great suffering after they die. I want so badly for you and all people to live for all eternity with love himself. I want so badly for you to experience love himself in your life right now. **I thirst for you to love Jesus.** I don't care who you are, what you have done or are doing; I want you to know the love of the one who is love. I thirst for your soul because I fear that many Americans falsely assume they are going to heaven. I believe that people are deceived in assuming that because they are basically "a good person" they are going to go to heaven. **Your soul may be in danger of hell.** I say this not out of judgment or condemnation, but rather out of love. Are you working out your salvation with fear and trembling? Or do you walk down the broad path that leads to destruction, thinking all the while that you are one of the few who have found the narrow path?

If you walk into the average church and start asking the Christians in that church about their lives, you will learn a few things about them. First, you will learn that they claim to love Christ and to love his people, but after further examination, I think that often you will find that they do not live these realities. They cannot possibly love Christ as they say they do, because they spend all their time with sports, electronics, computers, video games, movies, television, music, recreation, and laziness, and so little time is given to God in prayer. You will also learn that they can't truly love all of God's people because many of them are not actually concerned about helping the poor, or reaching out to the suffering, or sharing the Gospel with those who don't know Christ. These so-called Christians are not concerned about holiness and living their entire life for Jesus Christ. They're not concerned about setting time aside each day to love God and grow in a relationship with him. They definitely aren't concerned about the mission of bringing about the Kingdom of God.

Do you know what the modern American Christian is most concerned about? Comfort. That's right. Comfort. The modern American Christian wants to build a life of comfort for himself. He wants to get good grades and go to a good college so that he will get a good job and make lots of money. He wants to make lots of money not so that he can help to pull the poor out of their suffering or aid the Church in her missions, but rather, he wants money so that he can drive nice cars and live in nice homes, take comfortable vacations, enjoy expensive dinners and go to expensive sporting events. He wants money not to help the needs of others, but for the comforts of his own recreation and entertainment. Many American Christians are concerned with themselves — their own wants, their own desires, their own pleasures and comforts. If by chance they show concern for another, it is often because of some emotional warmth they get out of it and thus their outreach to others isn't even selfless, but selfish.

This is why Benedict tells us over and over again, **"You were not made for comfort. You were made for great-**

ness."

We have forgotten the important teaching of the Gospel of Matthew: "Enter through the narrow gate. For wide is the gate and broad is the road that leads to destruction, and many enter through it. But small is the gate and narrow the road that leads to life, and only a few find it." To be a disciple who follows Jesus means that you cannot live like the rest of the world lives.

The rest of the world lives in an overindulgent way. The rest of the world lives in a comfort- and pleasure-seeking way. American Christians act almost exactly like American non-Christians. Just compare the divorce rates, the contraception rates, the co-habitation rates., the pre-marital sex rates, and the abortion rates. They are practically the same. American Christians live in the same overindulgent homes and spend their money on the same great vacations as non-Christians. Look at the way they interact with their enemies. Christians are called to love their enemies, but the majority love those who love them and hate those who hate them — do not the pagans do the same? If you walk like the world, talk like the world, act like the world, listen to the perverse music of the world, watch the profane TV shows and movies of the world, dress immodestly like the world, have all the expensive and unnecessary electronics of the world, seek your own interests like the world, then what on earth makes you think you are on the narrow path? If only a few find the narrow path, if only a few dare to walk the narrow path, then wouldn't it be safe to assume that the vast majority of the world is on the path that leads to destruction?

I am not saying that all the world is going to hell, for I trust that the mercy of God is greater than our worldliness, but you must understand that being a good person isn't what gets you to heaven. Simply believing in God isn't enough to get you to heaven — even Satan acknowledges that Jesus is Lord. Calling yourself a Christian isn't what gets you to heaven either.

So what does get us to heaven? Jesus tells us the answer. "Not everyone who says to me, 'Lord, Lord,' will enter the kingdom of heaven, **but only the one who does the will of my Father who is in heaven."**

When you are confused as to how a disciple of Jesus Christ is supposed to live, don't look to the world and to the false prophets of this world. Look to Jesus. Open the Gospels and read them carefully. Find out what Jesus says and obey it. Ghandi hit the nail on the head when he said: "I like your Christ. I do not like your Christians. Your Christians are so unlike your Christ." **When will we stop acting like the rest of the world and start acting like Jesus Christ?**

If you want to stop assuming that you are going to heaven, if you want to be a weapon for righteousness, a true disciple, a revolutionary, a saint, then start *doing* the will of the Father in heaven. Walk down the narrow path. That means that you can't blend into the rest of the word. It's a *narrow* path — a path that fewer people choose to walk. The saints are the ones who walk down the narrow path. The true revolutionary must look radically different from the people of the world.

Yes, compared with the normal Christian you probably look pretty good. You may even look great. *Our problem isn't that we don't have a standard of holiness; our problem is that we set our standard of holiness according to the standards of the world instead of according to he who is the standard, Jesus Christ.* For Jesus says in Matthew 5:48, "Be perfect as your heavenly Father is perfect." Another way to say this is to be holy as your heavenly Father is holy. Our standard for how "good" we are, how well we are following Christ, cannot and should not be the world. Our standard must be the holiness of God himself.

Discipleship is not only about crying, 'Lord, Lord,' but it also requires walking the narrow path, following Christ the King down the path he walked.

It means loving the things that Jesus loves.

It means hating the things that Jesus hates.

It means living the way that Jesus lived.

LOVE WHAT JESUS LOVES, HATE WHAT JESUS HATES

Be real for just one minute: Do you honestly love what Jesus loves and hate what Jesus hates? Or are many of the things that you love the things that Jesus hates?

Look at your way of life; look at the way you live; look at the passions of your heart. What consumes your time? What consumes your thoughts? Is it Jesus? Or is he simply an accessory in your daily life?

Does your life reflect the lives of the saints and the life of Jesus Christ, or does it reflect the lives of those who live of the world? Let's spend some time examining our lives and truly asking ourselves if we are walking the narrow path.

Media

Are the movies and TV shows you watch the will of God? I promise that if they have sexual content and perverted humor, if they glorify sin, impure relationships, drinking or drugs, merciless killing and violence for the sake of violence, then these movies are not the will of God the Father. God hates the majority of the movies that we love because they glorify sin. They make sin look attractive. They make sin appear to lead to the happy life. Do not be deceived. Think long and hard about what movies and shows you watch. Would you watch these shows if Jesus were sitting next to you?

Is the music you listen to the will of God? Are the words that you sing in your car the words you will be singing before Christ the King for all eternity in heaven? It doesn't matter how much you like the melody or the rhythm — if the words do not bring glory to God or if the lives of those who sing the words do not bring glory to God, then what justifies this music? The Devil can clothe himself in all kinds of different appearances. Even if the lyrics of the music you listen to aren't bad, it is possible you simply spend too much time listening to music. Silence is the greatest worship before the almighty God. Do you have time for silence in your life?

Are the things you read the will of God? I am always amazed by the number of people who spend countless hours reading every sentence of a long fictional series but then fail to give their time to reading the voice of truth found in sacred Scripture. A man is often measured by the sum of the things he has read. Books affect our inmost being. Don't fill yourself with junk. Don't fill yourself with trivial nonsense. Read books that matter. Are the magazines you spend time reading worth reading? Or do they keep your mind focused on the passing things of this world and not the glory of heaven?

Are the video games you play the will of God? Is senseless blood and violence actually the will of God? Are video games that glorify killing, stealing, and beating really the will of God? Many of the video games people play fail to recognize the dignity of the human person. Be not mistaken. These video games can and do desensitize you.

Are the websites you view the will of God? If you are struggling with video sites that lead you to sin, you must take immediate action to cut this out of your life. That may mean removing the computer from your room, or having your parents put a password on the computer so you can't use it when they aren't home. Maybe this means putting a strong filter on your computer. Maybe that means asking someone to help you overcome these temptations. If you are struggling with this, take action. Repent and do what you need to do to avoid this sin.

Taming the Tongue

Are the jokes you laugh at and the things you speak the will of God?

"Death and life are in the power of the tongue!" (Proverbs 18:21)

"Let no evil talk come out of your mouths, but only such as is good for edifying, as fits the occasion, that it may impart grace to those who hear." (Ephesians 4:29)

"If a man who does not control his tongue imagines that he is devout, he is self-deceived." (James 1:26)

With the tongue we bless the Lord and Father, and with it we curse human beings who are made in the likeness of God.

Examine yourself. Do you need to cut out any forms of negative speech that are common in your life, such as using the Lord's name in vain, cussing, lying or exaggerating, boasting, self-deprecation, grumbling or complaining, perverted humor, gossip, ridicule, sarcasm, harsh voice tone, discouragement, retaliation, manipulation, belittling of others, judgment, and flirting?

Or is it possible that your tongue is silent when it should not be? "Do not refrain from speaking at the crucial time, and do not hide your wisdom." (Sirach 4:23)

"Do not let any unwholesome talk come out of your mouths, but only what is helpful for building others up according to their needs, that it may benefit those who listen." (Ephesians 4:29)

Instead of negativity, focus on all the good that can come forth from your tongue: affirmation, truth, encouragement, appreciation, evangelization, rejoicing (even in hardship), and of course, prayer and worship.

Money and Possessions

Everything you have is a gift from above. The Lord blessed you to be born into your current state of life. That was a generous act of mercy on his part. You had nothing to do with being born where you were born and in the family to which you were born. You had nothing to do with the shelter placed over your head. That was a gift from God.

Are the things you spend your money on the will of God the Father? Do you give generously to the Church and to the poor? Or is this something you think God expects only from your parents? Do you spend your money responsibly, or does all of your money go to selfish gain?

Is the amount of possessions, electronics, and clothes you have the will of God the Father? Do you have too much? Do you need everything you have, or do you confuse need and want too often? Are you too attached to the things of this world? Do you place too much happiness in these? Chances are, if you dress just like everyone else and have all the newest electronics that everyone else has, then you are probably walking down the broad road that leads to destruction.

The Lord calls all Christians to live a life of simplicity. Over and over again in the Gospels you see the Lord telling people that you cannot serve both God and money, that you need to give to the poor, that you need to be poor and simple yourself. Nowhere in the Gospels does it say that you can own all of the possessions of the world as long as you aren't attached to them. This is a modern lie and isn't the Gospel. In order to justify our sin, we have convinced ourselves that it is okay to drive the same cars, wear the same expensive clothes, have the same expensive possessions as everyone else in the world as long as we aren't "attached" to them. Where is that in the Gospel? These aren't the words of Jesus; these are the words of self-justifying sinners. Jesus tells us to be concerned with the needs of the poor, which means that we need to live a simple life so that we are more able to give.

What do you need to give up? Where do you need to simplify?

Are the clothes you wear the will of God the Father, or are they immodest? Immodesty reveals the sacredness that God has asked you to treasure and reserve for your spouse. It doesn't reveal too much; it reveals too little.

Time

Just as our money belongs to the Lord, so too does our time belong to the Lord. God is the author of time and he only gives us so much of it. I am constantly amazed by how busy the modern teenager is. Your time has been completely swept away in academics, sports, clubs, organizations, and expectations of others.

Is where you spend your time the will of God the Father? Jesus asks you to be committed to him and to the Kingdom of God. If our current commitments in life make it impossible to be committed wholeheartedly to Jesus and his kingdom, then chances are we are not on the narrow path. Something has got to give. If you don't have time to pray, something in your schedule has got to give.

What is it that keeps you from being completely committed to Jesus Christ? Whatever that thing is, I challenge you to cut it out of your life. If playing sports year-round keeps you from being committed, then cut some of that out. If being consumed by dance or band keeps you from being committed to Christ, then cut some of that out. If your friends are keeping you from being completely committed to Christ, then cut them out. If the amount of time you invest in a boyfriend or girlfriend keeps you from being committed, then cut that relationship off.

I would even go so far as to say that if maintaining a 3.5 or a 4.0 grade point average keeps you from being fully committed to Christ, then you need to get rid of that expectation. This doesn't mean be lazy in school, but it means that you need to start praying and being committed to Christ and entrust your academics to him. Seek first the Kingdom of God and then your academics.

Ultimately, the question to ask yourself is this: **What consumes your life?** If the answer isn't Jesus, something needs to change. The next chapter will teach you how to make that change.

TALK ABOUT IT.

(If reading with a group, use these questions for discussion.)

1. How hard do you strive for holiness? How can you strive harder?

2. What does it mean to "work out your salvation with fear and trembling?" (Philippians 2:12)

3. Do you strive to store up earthly treasure? Do you try to serve both God and money?

4. How much do you worry? About your clothes? About your future? About what others think about you?

5. What part of walking down the narrow path scares you?

6. What is the foundation that you are building your life on? Is your foundation strong? Are you the wise or foolish builder? Does your foundation need to change?

7. What consumes your life? If you were to evaluate your priorities based on what consumes your time and thoughts the most, what would they be?

8. What about the examination of conscience convicted you to change? (media, speech, money, possessions, time)

TAKE ACTION

ACTION STEP 1: Evaluate your favorite TV shows and resolve to cut out all the shows that are not the will of God the Father.

ACTION STEP 2: Evaluate the music you have on your iPod and the radio stations you listen to and resolve to delete all the songs or artists that are not the will of God the Father.

ACTION STEP 3: Go to confession and confess having exposed yourself to these things.

ACTION STEP 4: If you are struggling with pornography, write down a game plan on how to overcome this addiction. You're plan should include:

- When will you go to confession?

- What kind of a block will you put on your computer of TV?

- Who will you ask to hold you accountable?

ACTION STEP 5: Resolve to make God your first priority by waking up earlier each day and spending time in prayer. Now sure how to start a prayer life? Read the next chapter.

www.Holiness✝Revolution.com

5
THE PRAYER DARE

Pope Benedict XVI said this about prayer in one of his homilies: "Prayer is not optional, but rather a question of life or death. . . . Only the person who prays can enter into eternal life."

If prayer is a life-or-death matter, then we probably should start taking it a little more seriously. We should be concerned with prayer every moment of every day. The Holy Father is telling us that prayer is more important than food, water, and shelter. Prayer is our spiritual breath. You don't have to think in order to breathe, because the atmosphere exerts pressure on your lungs and essentially forces you to breathe. That's why it's more difficult to hold your breath than it is to breathe. In the same way, we live in a culture that exerts a ton of pressure on our lives. Failing to pray would be like failing to breathe. If we don't breathe, we will suffocate and die; if we don't pray, we will suffocate on our own sin. Benedict is telling us that prayer is so critical to the Christian way of life that it should be as normal and natural as breathing. And the Pope isn't being wimpy — he is saying that if we Christians don't pray, we are going to end up in hell. We are going to end up spiritually dead, without God.

We need prayer because we need God. "If God is necessary, prayer is necessary, for prayer is our spiritual lifeline to God. In prayer, we plug into God, the source of all good; we charge our spiritual batteries, we feed our souls. Without prayer our souls starve." *(Kreeft, Peter J. "Prayer." Catholic Christianity. San Francisco: Ignatius Press, 2001. 376)*

Prayer is an opportunity to quiet our souls and to encounter the living God. He who is the living God, he who is the beginning and the end, the Creator of heaven and earth, he who holds all things in existence, wants to encounter you, and wants you to encounter him. **He wants you to hear his voice, know his will, and walk in his ways.**

"Whether we realize it or not, prayer is the encounter of God's thirst with ours. God thirsts that we may thirst for him." (CCC 2560)

The more we neglect prayer, the more we separate ourselves from a relationship with Jesus, and thus, the more we will enter into sin, which is choosing the path of death. Prayer is meant to make us a saint — not just because we are doing the prayer, but because of what prayer does to us.

The purpose of prayer and the result of prayer is always conversion. Conversion means turning away from one thing and turning to another thing. It can't simply be turning away from. Instead of merely turning away from anger, we need to turn toward love. Instead of merely turning away from lust, we need to turn toward purity. From sloth to action. From pride to humility. From greed to selflessness. From materialism to simplicity. You get the point.

We need *conversion*. Initial conversion occurs when we start allowing God to turn our hearts more fully toward him. Continual conversion is the process that occurs throughout the rest of our lives as we continually let God transform and challenge us to greater holiness. We are never done growing, and thus **we are never done praying.** When we make it a habit to meet God every day in prayer, he begins to really *transform* and *revolutionize* our hearts. The more time we spend with him, the more like him we'll become.

If we can say that the purpose of prayer is conversion, then we could also say that the purpose of prayer is change. I would be so bold as to say that **prayer that fails to change us is not sincere prayer.** Our spiritual life depends on prayer. Our salvation depends on our spiritual life because we must constantly be molded and changed into the image of Jesus Christ. "Be perfect as your Heavenly Father is perfect." (Matthew 5:48) This is a lofty challenge from Jesus, and it is in prayer that he makes this challenge possible.

God desperately wants to change us. He wants us to be holy as he is holy, perfect as he is perfect. He wants us to reveal his goodness and his glory to this world. He wants to change our hearts, our minds, our souls, and our actions. "When you seek me with all your heart, you will find me with you, says the Lord, and I will change you." (Jeremiah 29:13)

And in this lies the real reason people don't pray: They are afraid of change. It's not that prayer is boring, or that God doesn't speak, or that it's too hard to stay focused, or even that we don't have time for it. If your prayer time is boring, it's because you hear the same thing every time you pray, and you never change. And so God continues telling you where you must change, day after day, after day, after day . . . but you fail to change! Of course it would be boring to listen to God repeat himself! If you start changing every day, then God will start speaking new realities to your heart.

If you say that God doesn't speak to you, I would challenge you and say that God does speak to you, but you are too afraid to listen to him speak. You're afraid of what changes God may be calling you to make in your life and so you run away from his voice. You're afraid of actually hearing his voice and so instead of listening to him speak, you tell yourself what you think God wants from you. You decide for yourself what God's will is for your life. Sound familiar? We all do it.

The excuse that we don't have time is the worst excuse of all. After all, God is outside of time; he is the Creator of time and space. If you asked the Creator of time and space to give you time to pray, would he not do so? In reality, you have time to pray; you just don't use your time well. Most of our time is consumed with meaninglessness, with noise, with distractions, and to be honest, with laziness. We act like we are busy, but the reality is, many of us are just lazy. Instead of praying, we choose to watch TV. Instead of praying, we choose to get online, or to talk on the phone, or to play video games.

So if you don't pray, stop making excuses and start giving God what he is due. Be honest with yourself — you probably don't pray because you're afraid to change; you're afraid of conversion. You don't pray because you think TV or the Internet is going to bring you more satisfaction in life than the God of heaven and earth. You don't pray because prayer makes you uncomfortable.

Be not afraid! Be not afraid of change and conversion. "Do not be afraid of the demands the Gospel of Christ places upon you." (Pope Benedict XVI) There is absolutely nothing to fear. Christ promises us everything, and he delivers. ***You can change.*** You can be the man or the woman you were created to be. You can be a person of prayer.

I DARE YOU TO PRAY

When you encounter the living God in prayer, you will change. And so I dare you to encounter him. I dare you to allow yourself to be changed. This is my Prayer Dare: **I dare you to spend real, substantial time with God in prayer from this day forth.** Not just a few seconds here and there, not just a ten-second prayer before dinner, or a Hail Mary before you drool on your pillow, but real, dedicated time. This is the secret to happiness. This is the secret to a life of joy and peace. This is the secret to becoming a saint. What does it mean to give dedicated time? Start with ten minutes, and each week, add five or ten minutes until you hit thirty minutes to an hour. Jesus himself asks us, "Will you not keep watch with me for one hour?" (Matthew 26:41)

The Prayer Dare:

Do it (every day)

Ask (where you need to be changed)

Respond (to what God is asking of you)

Expect (great things)

D: DO IT (EVERY DAY)

If prayer is a matter of life and death, you need to do it every day. Prayer must be a commitment like school or sports, or eating. So commit and stick to it! As our friend Yoda says, "Do. Or do not. There is no try." Wimps try — and wimpy Christians try to pray every day. Don't be a wimpy Christian. Pray.

The next time you're in the car, try turning off the radio and talking to God in the silence. Instead of watching one more TV show, or instead of killing time on the Internet, go to your room and open your Bible. In our society today, we are constantly surrounded by noise and distractions, so much so that we crowd out God's voice and we end up making all of our life's decisions instead of asking God about our life. Don't fill your life with so much noise and busyness that you are deaf to God's whisper saying, "I love you" and "I want you to serve me in great and wonderful ways."

Nothing is more important in your life than God. **If you're too busy to pray, then you're too busy!** Simply put, make time for prayer. Wake up earlier, drop an extracurricular, work fewer hours in the week, whatever it takes — after all, it is a matter of life or death. If we ask him, God will give us the grace to *make time* for prayer. It won't always be easy, but you have to decide how important prayer is going to be in your life. I have worked with countless high school students who have quit a sport or an extra-curricular to make more time for prayer and mission. It was that important to them. How important is it to you? If you dedicate yourself to daily prayer, the rest of your life will run much more smoothly. God will bless you for being faithful to him. When I am faithful to giving God the first fruits of my time, he is faithful in letting me get done all of my daily tasks.

Remember, prayer is hard work. You won't be a pro football player in a day, and you won't be a pro prayer in a day. Like anything, prayer takes a lot of time and commitment if we want to be good at it. It takes hard work and dedication. The saints were fervent in prayer, not lazy. Here is how you can form a habit of prayer to make sure you pray every day:

- **Set a Consistent Time.** Find a time in the day that you can dedicate to God, such as before school or before you go to sleep. It should be a time when you are alert and ready to give yourself to prayer.

- **Find a Consistent Place.** Find a set place to go that is free from distractions. Having a focal point such as a crucifix can help. You may even choose to set up a prayer altar in your bedroom.

- **Have a Prayer Plan.** Have a plan when you sit down for prayer. Maybe do the daily Mass readings or read through the Gospels. Maybe read the lives of the saints. Maybe you want to journal about your life and write letters to God.

- **Avoid Discouragement.** Didn't pray yesterday? Don't despair. "So you have failed? You have not failed; you have gained experience. Forward!" —Saint Josemaria Escriva

A: ASK (WHERE YOU NEED TO BE CHANGED)

Have you ever met the kind of person who talks, and talks, and talks? Whenever you are about to get a word in, he thinks of something else to say. She'll ask you questions, but not wait for answers. He'll share a thought but not listen to your thought. We all know a person or two like this, and we all know that talking to him or her can be frustrating.

Imagine how God feels. For so many of us, that is the kind of relationship we have with God. We say our Hail Marys and Our Fathers. We say our grace before meals and pray for help when we need it. We ask him questions, but we don't wait for answers. Often, our prayer is merely talk, talk, talk. When we pray, we can't simply go before God and do all the talking. We need to be carefully attentive to what God wants to say to us.

A big part of prayer is asking God to reveal to us where we need to change. We need to listen carefully for his voice, and in that, he will reveal to us how he wishes for us to be better molded into his image. God also wishes to speak his will to you. He wants to tell you what mission he has for you or what vocation he is calling you to live. Prayer is about listening to the voice of the Lord so that he can speak his will into our lives.

You can listen to him a number of ways:

- Read the Bible and meditate on its words, placing yourself in the scenes.

- Pray the Rosary and meditate on the life of Jesus.

- Pray before the Blessed Sacrament and allow God's presence to transform you.

- Keep a spiritual journal, in which you write dialogues with God and allow the Lord to direct your pen.

- Read the lives or works of the saints and hear God speak through them.

When you pray, ask God where you need to change and ask him to help you change.

R: RESPOND (TO WHAT GOD IS ASKING OF YOU)

The life of holiness is a funny and awkward thing. On the one hand, we don't make ourselves holy. It is God who sanctifies us. But on the other hand, God won't sanctify us if we aren't striving to sanctify ourselves. God the Father desperately wants to sanctify our souls through an outpouring of the Holy Spirit — but the catch is, we need to be open to the Holy Spirit working in and through us. **No one becomes holy passively.** Holiness takes hard work, dedication, and action. Ultimately, if we really want to be holy, we need to not only listen to what God is asking of us, but we also need to respond with action.

One of the most powerful phrases I've ever heard is the simple two-word sentence "Love acts." When I heard this phrase, I was at a point in my relationship with God where I was led mainly by emotions. I followed God and "loved" God primarily because it excited me, fulfilled me, and made me happy. See the problem here? It was largely about me and not about him. I realized that if I was going to say, "I love you, Lord," that also meant, "I will take action for you, Lord."

Love acts, and if prayer is a loving union between God and man, then prayer too must act. After we hear the voice of God directing us to change and directing us toward his will for our life, then the only loving response is to strive our hardest to change.

The question remains: What should our response look like? Let's be honest, as young kids, when our parents asked us to do something, we may have responded, but typically we didn't respond virtuously. We would do what they asked, but whine and drag our feet the entire time. Instead of doing it as best we could, we would do it only halfway. When we respond to the will of God, we should do so like the Blessed Mother Mary.

When the angel Gabriel appeared to Our Lady and revealed to her that she would conceive the Son of God, she didn't freak out and say to the angel that if she was seen in public as an unwed pregnant woman she would be stoned to death. She didn't make an excuse as to why she wasn't good enough or wasn't the right person for the job. She didn't complain that it would be too difficult and lead to too much pain. Instead, Mary's response was very simple: "I am the handmaid of the Lord, be it done unto me according to Thy Word." (Luke 1:38) The word handmaid can also be translated as "servant." Mary acknowledges that she is the servant of the Lord, and as his servant, she responds without question or excuse, but with joy and humility. Likewise, our response should be one of joyful service. We should respond to the word of the Lord in our lives joyfully ready to serve the Lord as best we possibly can.

E: EXPECT (GREAT THINGS)

What great things can you expect when you pray? You can expect love. You can expect security. You can expect to hear the quiet whisper of Jesus. You can expect answers. You can expect results.

What is the deepest longing of the human heart? Love. Love is our deepest longing. We all long to be loved and accepted unconditionally. We all long to have someone who will never leave us, no matter what. In Jesus, this longing is fulfilled. Jesus promised us over and over again in Scripture that he would never leave us. "Behold, I will be with you always, even until the end of time." (Matthew 28:20)

In prayer, we come into a deep and loving union with Jesus Christ. The more we pray, the more this love will grow and deepen. We will find ourselves caught up passionately with Jesus Christ, thinking about him and his kingdom all day long. There will come a point where your love for him is so deep that you won't want to stop praying. Ten minutes won't be enough. Neither will thirty. Nor an hour. Many of the saints experienced this kind of prayer. Saint Teresa of Avila was often caught up in states of ecstasy that she said were times of indescribable pleasure. Saint John of the Cross was so moved by love of God in prayer that he would grab the statue of the infant Jesus in his arms and dance with it. Saint Therese of Lisieux described prayer as a "surge of the heart."

What? Prayer is a surge of the heart? This definition of prayer is vastly different from the prayer we see most Catholics engaged in during Mass, in which they are drifting in and out of sleep, or if they manage to stay awake, their eyes are glazed over with boredom. This isn't how it has to be — God offers us more than this! He wishes our prayer to be an amazing encounter of love. So expect great things when you pray. Expect this amazing relationship with Jesus to come — maybe not today, and maybe not tomorrow, but be persistent in daily prayer, and wait for the surge of your heart.

"Ask and it will be given to you; seek and you will find; knock, and the door will be opened to you. For everyone who asks, receives; and the one who seeks, finds; and to the one who knocks, the door will be opened." (Matthew 7:7–8)

When we pray, we should *expect* results. We should expect that God will answer our prayers, that he will give us the grace to change, and that he will heal us and others. But remember, we pray so that we can be changed. We don't pray so that we can change God's mind. Asking him for things means that we are asking him for the grace to deal with his will. When I was young, my grandpa got really sick. I prayed and prayed and prayed for him to get better, because I wanted to be able to go fishing and camping with him again, but after years of a slow and painful illness, my grandpa died. As a seventh-grader, I felt let down by God and I was really angry with him. Why didn't he answer my prayers? Why didn't my grandpa get better? And then, at the funeral Mass, I realized that God *did* answer my prayers. My grandpa would be much healthier in heaven than he ever would have been here on earth. Jesus answered my prayers and allowed my grandpa to get better; he just didn't answer them how I'd thought he would. When we ask something of God, we are asking, "Thy will be done," not "Our will be done."

TALK ABOUT IT.

(If reading with a group, use these questions for discussion.)

1. Do you treat prayer as a matter of life and death? Why or why not?

2. When you pray, are you afraid to change? Why or why not?

3. In your own conversion, what are examples of areas that you have turned away from sin and turned towards virtue? What are areas that this conversion still needs to happen?

4. What is your current prayer life like? Where is God asking you to go?

5. What are obstacles to your prayer life? How can you overcome these?

6. When you pray, do you "expect great things?"

7. What kind of a prayer resolution will you make? Who will you ask to keep you accountable to keeping this resolution?

TAKE ACTION

ACTION STEP 1: Write up a game plan for your new prayer life. What commitments are you making? What time of day will you pray? Where will you pray? What will you use in prayer? (Scripture, journal, books, etc.)

ACTION STEP 2: Write a letter to yourself communicating the commitments you are making today. Give this letter to a parent, friend, youth minister, or religious teacher and ask them to mail it to you in six months. Six months later, you will get a nice little reminder of how the Lord was working in your life today and the need to keep praying.

ACTION STEP 3: Fold a piece of paper in half. On one side of the paper write down all the intercessions you would like to offer to God, both for yourself and for others. On the other side of the paper, write down everything that you are thankful for. Use this paper in your prayer time each day so that you remember to pray for those in need and to thank God for all He has done for you. Don't forget to keep adding to the lists each week.

www.Holiness Revolution.com

6
THE WEAPONS OF A SAINT

The saints know that they wage the revolution of holiness not with their own power but with the power from on high. They know that the revolution of holiness is a *spiritual* revolution and thus it requires spiritual weapons. If you wish to revolutionize your heart, you must be sure to arm yourself for the fight. The goal of this chapter is simple: to equip you with the weapons you need in order to fight in the revolution of holiness.

"Finally, be strong in the Lord and in his mighty power. Put on the full armor of God so that you may be able to stand firm against the tactics of the devil. For our struggle is not against flesh and blood but with the principalities, with the powers, with the world rulers of this present darkness. . . . Therefore, **put on the armor of God, so that when the day of evil comes, you may be able to stand your ground."** (Ephesians 6:10–13)

"For though we live in the world, we do not wage war as the world does. The weapons we fight with are not the weapons of the world. On the contrary, they have divine power to demolish strongholds." (2 Corinthians 10:3–4)

The weapons the Blessed Trinity has given to us are endless, but some of the key weapons I want to talk about are: the holy Eucharist, reconciliation, the Church, community, the Blessed Mother Mary, and the Holy Spirit.

THE HOLY EUCHARIST

Not too long ago, a joyful but frustrated teenage girl named Jenny came to me with a question. She asked if it was okay to call herself Catholic even though she wasn't really able to connect to God. She looked at me and she said, "I've never been able to connect with God — is that normal?"

I assured her that it is normal for people to struggle with connecting to God, but there are things that we can do to help ourselves connect with him. I didn't know Jenny at all — she had watched a documentary on A&E that I was on and stalked me on Facebook to find my number — so the first question I asked her was whether or not she went to Mass every week. When she said no, I immediately knew why she wasn't "connecting" with God. I said to her, "How can you expect to connect with God if you aren't spending time with God at Mass?" Her response nearly made me cry. Jenny said to me, "I don't understand how a piece of blessed bread can help me connect with God." I realized then and there just how much we as Catholics sometimes take the Eucharist for granted.

The Eucharist is Jesus's body, blood, soul, and divinity. We believe that when we receive the Eucharist, we are literally receiving *all* of Jesus, *all* of God. The Eucharist isn't a symbol or a reminder of God; *it really is God*. God enters our bodies. God literally is physically present inside us. The Eucharist is so much more than "blessed bread," because it is God himself. If we want to connect with God, what better way than to bring him into your body? Mass is a taste of heaven. In heaven you will be in God's presence at all times and you will share an intimate union with Christ. Mass is a foreshadowing of heaven here on earth. At every Mass, heaven and earth literally smash together and those in heaven come to us on earth, and we spend time together as the one body of Christ, and one communion of saints.

When we receive Holy Communion, we do not receive blessed bread. We receive the body, blood, soul, and divinity of Jesus Christ. While the physical properties of bread and wine remain, the essence of the bread and wine become Jesus's body and blood. His body and blood are veiled by the physical appearance and properties of bread and wine out of love for us so that we can receive him as often as possible. Sound unbelievable? Well, if Jesus could rise from the dead, why couldn't he do this? He is God, and God is unbelievable.

Every revolutionary needs to be radically Eucharistic. Our spiritual life must be rooted in and strengthened by the Blessed Sacrament. Why?

Other food, when consumed, becomes us — the nutrients become our flesh. But when we receive the holy Eucharist, it transforms us. We become more like what we have received. We become more like Christ. So tell me, can a revolutionary fighting in this spiritual battle of holiness survive without the Eucharist? Will we have victory without the Eucharist being our source of life? As we wage war amid the culture in which we live, as we live as missionaries in the world, Mass becomes our oasis.

There is no better way to start your day as a soldier of Christ than Mass. At Mass, we receive our marching orders through the readings and the preaching. At Mass, we learn how to bring a change to the world. At Mass, we approach the throne of Christ the King, and we receive our king. **We consume the body of Christ in order to *be* the body of Christ.** The Eucharist strengthens us to live as Christ in the world — to be his hands, his feet, his heart, his lips, and his love. Receive and be.

If we aren't present to Christ in the Eucharist, then we need to change our lives. At the bare minimum, we need to get to Sunday Mass. But I believe that the Lord wants even more from his revolutionaries. Wake up early. Go to daily Mass before school. Find a church near you that has a daily Mass after school. Do what it takes. (You can find the daily Mass times of churches near you at masstimes.org).

Another way to embrace the Eucharistic love of Jesus Christ is to spend time in his presence through Eucharistic adoration. If you have never heard about adoration, it is when the Eucharist is exposed in a sacred vessel, called a monstrance. In adoration, we are able to sit in the presence of God and simply adore him. We are face-to-face with Jesus and allow his grace to soak into our souls.

How often do we really stop and think about the staggering truth that the *God of the universe* humbles himself and comes to us under the appearance of a simple piece of bread? **There is no greater proof of God's love for us in this world than that of the Eucharist.**

The majority of Christians believe that we have to wait for heaven to be in Christ's presence. But as Catholics, we know that is simply not the case. Jesus is as present in the Eucharist as he was two thousand years ago on the dusty streets and green hilltops of the Middle East. Are we taking advantage of this enormous blessing? Jesus Christ quietly waits for us in every tabernacle and monstrance throughout the world. He is humbly present to us under the appearance of bread and wine, but *are we present to him?*

"Each time we look upon Jesus in the Blessed Sacrament, he raises us up into deeper union with himself, opens up the floodgates of his merciful love to the whole world, and brings us closer to the day of his final victory 'where every knee will bend and proclaim Jesus Christ as Lord.' The coming of Jesus to us in the Eucharist is assurance of his promise of final victory: 'Behold, I come to make all things new.'" (Blessed Mother Teresa of Calcutta)

"Neither theological knowledge nor social action alone is enough to keep us in love with Christ unless both are preceded by a personal encounter with him. Theological insights are gained not only from between two covers of a book, but from two bent knees before an altar. The Holy Hour becomes like an oxygen tank to revive the breath of the Holy Spirit in the midst of the foul and fetid atmosphere of the world." (Archbishop Fulton J. Sheen)

Seek out adoration. Seek out his love.

To find opportunities for adoration near you, go to:
http://www.therealpresence.org/chap_fr.htm

RECONCILIATION

The sacrament of reconciliation may be the most underused and underappreciated weapon of holiness we have. Often, we treat confession as a burden rather than as a gift. We treat it as a consequence of sin, as opposed to a vehicle of overcoming sin. With great joy, I can profess that confession frees me from the chains and bondage of sin, and enables me to live in the freedom of Christ.

In high school I struggled with a number of sins, many of which I was ashamed and embarrassed to confess. For years, I would go to confession and confess only the sins that were easy or that I wasn't ashamed to confess. My biggest sins were kept secret. One night, I was convicted in prayer that I had hid from Jesus's present in the confessional for far too long. He was asking me to confess *everything*. And so I listened to what God asked of me. As I sat down in the confessional, with my knees shaking, I confessed my first sin: "Forgive me Father, for I have sinned. The first sin I would like to confess is that I have never been completely honest in the confessional." The priest laughed, cracked his fingers, and said, "Oh, this is going to be fun." As I proceeded to confess the sins that I had kept in the dark for so long, the priest was not angry or judgmental; instead, he was filled with joy. He was so joyful that after so long I had finally come running to the merciful arms of Jesus Christ. When I was finished, he looked me in the eyes, and he said that Jesus loved me with an everlasting love. He said that I was free from my sins and I was ready to start a new life in Christ.

"Thus the nations shall know that I am the Lord, says the Lord God, when in their sight **I prove my holiness through you** . . . I will sprinkle clean water upon you to cleanse you from all of your impurities, and from all your idols I will cleanse you. I will give you a new heart and place a new spirit within you, taking from your bodies your stony hearts and giving you natural hearts." (Ezekiel 36:23b, 24–26)

You see, the beautiful thing about the sacrament of reconciliation is that even in our impurity, even in our filth, Jesus takes us into his arms and cleanses us. He replaces our stony, sinful hearts with his sacred heart. He allows us to be restored to complete union with him. And he does all of this because he wants to *prove his holiness through us*. In the Gospels, Jesus doesn't call the noblest of men. He doesn't call the high priests and the scribes. He calls sinners. He calls a woman caught in the act of adultery. He calls the tax collector, a thief. He calls Peter, who denies him three times. He calls James, Andrew, and the others, who run away when he is arrested. It pleases Jesus to call sinners to himself, because it is through sinners that he is able to *prove his holiness to the nations*. The greater the conversion, the more glory God receives. **If we are healed in our brokenness, then it is he who is glorified.** If Jesus can build his Church upon a poor fisherman who denies him three times, then there is hope for us.

I received such freedom from reconciliation. The sins that had held me captive for much of my life no longer had any hold on me. The confessional not only gives us the grace of forgiveness, but it also gives us the grace to overcome the sins we confess. After the confession in which I told the priest *all* of my sins, over the course of the next year, I overcame, through the grace of God, many of those sins that I had struggled with for so many years. **Confession gifts us the grace to overcome our sin — the grace of victory!**

Years later, I have new sins that I take to the Lord month after month in the confessional. Confession reminds me that I need a Savior, that I can't do this on my own. It reminds me that I am broken, and that I constantly fail in my service to God the Father and Christ the King. But it also reminds me that no matter how many times I fail, and **no matter how many times I have to confess the same stupid sin, I have a God who loves me no matter what.** No sin, no failing, can ever separate me from the love of God. I know that I am not yet perfect, but I also know that the grace of God can make me perfect.

Brothers and sisters, if you are struggling with sins in your life and you have not yet taken them to the confessional, you are missing out on the grace that sets us free! Do not underestimate the power of this sacrament. And do not use the excuse that you don't need to confess your sins to a priest in order to be forgiven. If Jesus didn't want us to go to the priest to receive forgiveness and healing, he would have never told the apostles, "Whose sins you forgive are forgiven them." (John 20:23)

The reality is, when we confess our sins to a priest, we are confessing our sins to Jesus. The priest acts *in persona Christi,* meaning he acts "in the person of Christ." It is Christ who forgives and it is Christ who heals. The priest, however, has a second role. He represents Christ, but he also represents the body of Christ, the Church. Every sin we commit not only hurts our relationship with God, but it hurts everyone in this world, because sin hurts this world. And so, we not only need to ask God for forgiveness, but we need to ask the people of God for forgiveness. The priest, acting in the person of Christ, reconciles us to God the Father and to the people of this world whom we have hurt.

The last thing I wish to say is this: **There is no shame in being a sinner.** Do not allow your sinfulness to turn into despair, and do not be so prideful as to think that you are capable of overcoming your sin on your own. When you sin, the best thing you can do is recognize that it is fitting for a sinner to sin and for a savior to save. If we were perfect, we would not need a savior. Do not allow sin to tear you down. Instead, allow your weakness to build you up. What do I mean by this? Even if you fall into the same sin a hundred times and confess it a hundred times, rejoice in the fact that you are a sinner in need of a savior. Only the person who knows he needs to be saved will beg for the gift of salvation.

Don't let pride, fear, shame, or guilt hold you back. No sin is bigger than the mercy of God. Jesus is ready and he is waiting in the confessional. Without this grace, how can we ever overcome the sins that hold us captive from the life we were meant to live?

If you want to get to a destination as quickly as you can without getting lost, you are going to use a map. The more accurate the map, the more likely you are to arrive at your destination. If you look at the map and pridefully think that you are smarter than the map, thus ignoring it, most likely you will end up extremely lost and wishing you had been more obedient.

If you wish to build a strong and sturdy house with as few errors as possible, you are going to use a blueprint. The blueprint for the house tells you exactly what you need to do in order to have the most success. Imagine deciding to ignore the blueprint here and changing things up there — what do you think will happen to the final product of the house? Depending on how big the changes are that you made, your adaptations could prove disastrous, causing the house to crumble to the ground.

Where am I going with these two analogies?

The holy Catholic Church *is* the road map to salvation and the blueprint of holiness. Jesus Christ entrusted to the apostles the Church and promised us that he would never leave us. The Church and Christ are one; you cannot have the one without the other. To say that you can have Christ without the Church is to say that you can have the head without the body or the groom without the bride. Without a body, the head cannot function. Without a bride, the bridegroom has no beloved. If this is true, imagine what it means about the road map to salvation and the blueprint of holiness.

If we want salvation, we need the Church. If we want to be holy, we need the Church. If we think we don't need a map and we make ourselves the master of our destination, surely we will be lost in the storms of life and fall away from the truth of Jesus Christ, which ultimately could have eternal consequences. If we ignore the divine builder and build with our own knowledge and strength, we will make mistakes and the house *will* tumble down.

There is a new popular phrase among Christians: "It's not about religion; it's about the relationship," meaning that Jesus doesn't care about the structural Church and the hierarchy; he only cares about the relationship you individually have with him. I have heard people say that Jesus hates religion because it is too institutional and institutions corrupt people.

Do not buy into this modern heresy. **Religion enables and strengthens the relationship.** Without the Church, there would be no baptism, no Eucharist, no forgiveness of sins, and no moral truth to guide us. Without religion there would be no Bible, because the canon of sacred Scripture was organized and put together by the Catholic Church under the inspiration of the Holy Spirit. If we follow the logic that we do not need the Church, we ultimately make ourselves God.

If there is no Church to interpret truth and to interpret sacred Scripture, then ultimately we are left to do this on our own. We individually interpret truth for ourselves, and in doing so, we make ourselves God. If I read the Bible and have no one to tell me what is meant by these words, I can easily fall into error. Jesus promised an advocate, a helper, the Holy Spirit. This Spirit leads and guides the Church in the infallible interpretation of sacred Scripture and tradition such that the Church cannot err. The Church is without error on matters of faith and morals not because of the human element of the Church, which of course is filled with sinners, but rather because of the divine element of the Church, the ongoing inspiration and guidance of the Holy Spirit. Left on our own, without the Spirit's guidance on matters of faith and morals, surely we miss the fullness of truth. It is true that Christ gives all Christians the gift of the Holy Spirit, but the Spirit works in a unique way in the Church that he does not in our individual lives.

For years the Catholic Church's teachings on papal primacy, papal infallibility, and apostolic succession have been questioned by many.

When I was in high school, I often thought to myself, "Who is the Church to tell me how to live my life?" and "Who is the Church to tell me right from wrong? I can figure that out on my own." I would attack the authority of the pope in our religion classes, saying, "An old celibate guy in Rome has no ability to speak to my life." I remember mocking my mother's obedience to the Church's teaching, saying that she had no ability to think for herself. And so, as a sixteen-year-old, I was convinced that I knew right from wrong. I was convinced that I had it all figured out and I didn't need the Church to help me. I was the driver who threw the map out the window and was picking which streets and highways to go on myself. I was the builder who rejected the architect's blueprint and went about building on my own knowledge.

I bought into the lie of relativism, picking and choosing truths for myself. I rejected the teachings of the Church that I wanted to reject and accepted the teachings that I wanted to accept. I remember at one point in high school I sat up in my bedroom and started drafting the guidelines of my own church in a small notebook. I wrote a number of different moral beliefs that my church would accept and some things that we wouldn't accept. I wrote a new creed that my church would profess and started to plan how I would run my church services so that they weren't quite as boring as I thought Mass was. All of this sounds crazy, doesn't it?

But think about this for one minute: Aren't there a ton of people who have done this in the past? Think about the hundreds and thousands of different Protestant churches, all teaching and believing different things, based on the beliefs of the pastor. Any person can start his or her own Christian church and teach that Christians should live this way and believe these truths. The problem with all of this is that people, not God, are telling us how Christians should live and what Christians should believe. Why would I want to listen to another person tell me what to believe about God, when God himself has already promised to tell us through the Church? The Church, in her two thousand years of inspiration from the Holy Spirit, has a wealth of knowledge that we simply cannot have as individuals. Individual Christian churches may have some truth, but we as Catholics have the *fullness* of truth!

Saint Paul speaks of the household of God being "the church of the living God, the pillar and foundation of truth." (1 Timothy 3:15) If the Church is the pillar and foundation of truth, and we are searching for truth, where else should we seek truth other than the teachings of the Church?

You may not understand all of the Church's teachings. If this is the case, I encourage you to do two things. First, pray that the spirit of understanding will enlighten your mind and heart to believe the fullness of truth. Join in the prayer of Scripture: "I do believe, help my unbelief." (Mark 9:24) Second, seek out the answers to your questions.

The Church teaches us everything we need to know in order to become a saint. The Church teaches us the morals we need to follow in order to become a saint. Through the Church, God gives us all the grace we need to become a saint. The Church is a gift and a blessing. Don't be so prideful to think you don't need the Church. She is here to help us along the road to salvation. She herself paves the road and clears all the hurdles placed in our path.

COMMUNITY

Another powerful weapon in the Holiness Revolution and the revolution of your own heart is community. As we talked about earlier, Jesus established a Church in order to help us grow in holiness. The Church is not merely a bunch of doctrines and beliefs, but it is *also the body of Christ,* the people of God. Christ did not intend for us to be lone rangers, living the Christian life alone. We are a people who have been brought together to help one another grow in holiness, change the world, and ultimately get to heaven.

The tremendous importance of Christian community is demonstrated by the simple fact that God is a community. The Blessed Trinity is a community of persons: Father, Son, and Holy Spirit. They exist as such a close community that they are literally three distinct divine persons and yet one God. The unity of the Christian community is meant to model the oneness of the Blessed Trinity. The Catholic Church, though it is made up of thousands of different parishes and millions of different Catholic people, exists as the one body of Christ, and we, her members, are united under one faith, one creed, and one liturgy, one Lord of all.

You cannot be a lone ranger. **You cannot become holy by yourself.** "As iron sharpens irons, so does one person sharpen another." (Proverbs 27:17) Christians help make other Christians holy. In my ten years of youth ministry I am convinced that **the single most important thing to the faith of a young disciple is community.** You are the people you hang out with. If you hang out with a bunch of people who are profane and perverse, who don't live moral lives, sooner or later you will be profane and perverse, and start falling more and more into immorality. On the other hand, if you surround yourself with other faithful Christians who are striving eagerly for the heart of Jesus and the service of his kingdom, you will find that your time becomes consumed with prayer, service, and revolution.

"A faithful friend is a sturdy shelter; he who finds one finds a treasure." (Sirach 6:14)

"Two are better than one; because they have a good reward for their labor. For if they fall, the one will lift up his fellow: but woe to him that is alone when he falls; for he has not another to help him up." (Ecclesiastes 4:9–11)

An army of one will be crushed. If you are trying to do this on your own, stop everything you are doing and beg Christ the King to bring other warriors into your life to fight with you, to strengthen you, and to help you revolutionize your life and the lives of others. Be persistent in this prayer until it has been answered.

BLESSED MOTHER MARY

The Blessed Mother Mary is by far one of the most powerful weapons we have in this spiritual fight. Saint Pio said that "the Rosary is *the weapon*" and Pope Pius IX said, "Give me an army praying the Rosary and I will conquer the world!" Simply put, Mary is a force to be reckoned with.

Why is Mary such a powerful force?

We all know the story of creation and the story of the fall. Man and woman were created in the image of God in the Garden of Eden, enjoying perfect harmony with God and with nature. And then, Adam and Eve choose to eat the forbidden fruit; they choose disobedience over holiness, pride over unity with God. When God finds them hiding from him out of shame, he foretells the pain and suffering that will result from their disobedience.

But immediately after Adam and Eve sin, God promises to send a Savior. Man rejected God, but God does not reject man. Instead, God promises Adam and Eve and all mankind that he will send a Savior to heal the brokenness caused by our disobedience. He condemns the serpent: "I will put enmity between you and the woman, between your offspring and hers; He will strike at your head, while you strike at his heel." (Genesis 3:15) Who is the woman? The Church has long held that the woman spoken of here is the image of all women, the Blessed Mother Mary, because it is her offspring, Jesus Christ, who crushes the head of the serpent upon the cross of Calvary.

Jesus and Mary are often referred to as the new Adam and the new Eve. Immediately after the Fall, instead of rejecting man and leaving us to fight for ourselves, God places *enmity* between the serpent and the new Adam and Eve. The word *enmity* means complete and total separation. If both Jesus and Mary have enmity toward the serpent, then we could say that both have complete and total separation from Satan, and thus from sin. While Adam and Eve chose to disobey the will of God, the new Adam and the new Eve choose perfect obedience to the will of God. Just as one man and one woman fall away from God, God uses one man and one woman to restore union with the Father.

And so why is Mary a force to be reckoned with? In her, we find a human person who lives with complete and total separation from the power of sin. Because of this, she is gloriously raised to reign with Christ the King as his queen and mother. The Devil cannot have any influence over her because she is full of God's grace. Likewise, the Devil has no power over her prayers. When she intercedes for us, we can be sure that these prayers will be received and answered by her son. What obedient son would refuse to do what his mother asks of him?

What does Mary do?

Late in my senior year of high school, I desired more than anything a relationship with Jesus. I wanted to be holy. I wanted to know and love Jesus. But there was one major problem: I didn't know how to pray. At this crossroads, I picked up the Rosary. Day after day, sometimes multiple times a day, I drove to a local Marian grotto and prayed the Rosary. The Blessed Mother Mary taught me how to pray. She taught me to love her son. She allowed me to learn what it meant to be a Christian man. Mary placed within me the desire to be a saint and the desire to "Shine like the stars in this corrupt and depraved generation." (Philippians 2:15)

Mary is unique in her humility. She doesn't seek our prayers and our veneration for her own sake. Rather, she seeks them for the sake of her son's glory. The goal of Marian devotion is simply to love Jesus more and to love him with the heart of Mary. The amazing spiritual reality taking place when you give Mary your heart is that she gives you her heart in return. We no longer love Jesus with our imperfect and sinful heart, but now we are able to love him with the immaculate heart of Mary. This makes any offering we give to Jesus exponentially greater. When Jesus receives our prayers, he receives them through the immaculate heart.

This is precisely what happened to me and to countless other Christians. Mary led me to her son. She taught me how to love him, what to say to him, and what it meant to imitate him. If you are struggling in your prayer life or your relationship with God, I urge you to turn to the Blessed Mother and simply see what happens.

THE HOLY SPIRIT

I humbly suggest there is no greater weapon in the revolution of holiness than the Holy Spirit. However, even though he is the most powerful weapon we could have in the revolution of our hearts, he is also the most underestimated. After all, how is a wimpy little dove really going to help us win a revolution over sin and Satan?

Understand this: With, in, and through the Holy Spirit, we live the Christian life with the strength of God as opposed to our own strength. The gift of the Holy Spirit is the gift of God stirred up within us.

A common misunderstanding about the Holy Spirit is that he is some kind of cosmic force or supernatural power that is beamed into us at baptism and confirmation; but in reality, the Holy Spirit is not a force or a power, he's not a wind or a dove, and he's not even a cool tongue of fire. The Holy Spirit is a divine person. He is the third divine person of the Blessed Trinity and because of this, we can have a relationship with him just like we can with God the Father and God the Son. But how? How do we have a relationship with the Holy Spirit? The truth is, you already have it! Through the sacrament of baptism, the Holy Spirit established the relationship between you and the Blessed Trinity. In the sacrament of confirmation, he strengthened that relationship. In the holy Eucharist, he nourishes and deepens the relationship. And in the sacrament of reconciliation, he heals and restores the relationship.

Ultimately, the Holy Spirit is given to us to sanctify us and make us holy. It is because of him that we overcome sin, live a life of virtue, and are able to be disciples who proclaim the Gospel to the world. Without him, we remain distant from God and separated from the love of the Blessed Trinity.

Earlier we spoke of being men and women who strive for sanctity, who settle for nothing less than living as saints. It is precisely the Holy Spirit who makes all of this possible. Without him, we cannot be holy. With him, we are sanctified and strengthened to live as perfect Christians. Jesus could not have commanded, "Be perfect as your heavenly Father is perfect," without also giving us the gift of the Holy Spirit. It is through living a life in the Spirit that we live a life of divine grace and power.

The Spirit is powerfully at work in all of the sacraments; however, I want to look more closely at what the Holy Spirit does in us through baptism and confirmation.

The Sacrament of Baptism

Baptism is so incredible! In this sacrament, we are plunged into the waters, die with Christ, and are raised out of the waters in order to rise with Christ and share in his victory over sin and death. We find new life in Christ, and original sin is blotted out while sanctifying grace is bestowed. We are incorporated into the Church and are made adopted sons and daughters of the Father. We are imparted with a spiritual seal that marks our soul as belonging to Christ for all of eternity. **We are made light for the world's darkness.** We put on Christ. We receive the theological virtues of faith, hope, and love. We receive the gifts of the Holy Spirit. We become temples of the Holy Spirit.

Whenever we witness a baptism, we should be cheering and hollering like crazed fans at a sporting event, "for you were once darkness, but now you are light in the Lord. Live as children of light." (Ephesians 5:8)

How beautiful and glorious is that!

The point is, there is something else that the sacrament of baptism does for the Christian that is often overlooked and underappreciated, so much so that the Second Vatican Council declared that this understanding needed to be emphasized and embraced more in the contemporary Church.

In baptism, we become *Christian*, meaning that we are "anointed" by the Holy Spirit. The word *Christ* means "God's anointed one." A Christian is not merely a follower of Jesus; he is a sharer in Christ's anointing. This anointing of the Holy Spirit is a threefold anointing that invites and obliges us to share in the very mission of Christ, who is priest, prophet, and king.

Did you catch that? **Baptism incorporates you into the mission of Jesus Christ, the mission of bringing all souls to the Father and ushering in the Kingdom of God.** You are invited and obliged to share in the mission of the redeemer of the world! It is the Holy Spirit who bestows this mission upon you and carries it out through you. It is the Holy Spirit who anoints you as priest, prophet, and king.

Jesus's priestly anointing is manifested in his call to be the suffering servant. The many sacrifices of the priest in the Old Covenant never sufficed fully for the sins of the people of God. Jesus, the eternal high priest, is himself the sacrifice that ends all atonement sacrifices.

The Spirit anoints us as priest as well. Our priestly anointing calls us to a life of sacrifice. We are anointed to live a sacrificial life of dying to self in union with the cross of Christ and living with a resurrected joy. We as priests are called to place our own sinfulness on the altar as a sacrifice to the Trinity. The only thing we can give the Blessed Trinity that they have not already given to us is our own sin. This is the only thing that is truly ours, and this we must sacrifice.

Jesus's prophetic anointing is manifested in the way in which he proclaims the coming of the Kingdom of God. In this, he speaks the will of God the Father in all circumstances.

Our prophetic anointing calls us to speak the will of the Father, and like Christ, to proclaim the Kingdom of God in all circumstances. We are called to a life of discipleship and evangelization.

Jesus's kingly anointing is manifested most fully in the washing of the disciples' feet. It is here that he displays that his kingship is not of power and control, but of humility and service. The splendor of his kingship is marked by his holiness.

Our kingly anointing is that which empowers us to humbly be a servant to all. Our kingly rule is a rule over our very selves through the fruit of self-control so that we may declare authority over our sin, constantly growing in virtue and aiming to share completely in the holiness of Christ. **His anointing has made us holy!**

Through this anointing as priest, prophet, and king, we share in the same glorious and sacrificial mission of our Lord Jesus Christ We are able to share in the saving work of the Trinity

Life in the Spirit is manifested in the Christian through the fruits of the Holy Spirit: love, peace, joy, patience, generosity, kindness, faithfulness, gentleness, and self-control. Are those fruits in your life?

The Sacrament of Confirmation

Prepare yourself, because I am about to go on my soapbox. Nothing frustrates me more than the hours and hours we waste preparing young people for the sacrament of confirmation, while failing to actually teach them about confirmation. If you asked the average Catholic what confirmation is, most likely she would tell you it is the sacrament by which a person *confirms* the faith her parents choose for her when she was a baby, making it her own.

The problem with this is that it makes the recipient of the sacrament, not the giver of the sacrament, the focus. It makes confirmation out to be a Protestant version of "making Jesus your personal Lord and Savior." We are called to confirm our baptismal faith every morning. We confirm our baptismal faith each time we go to Mass and proclaim the Creed. We confirm our baptismal faith with every choice we make.

Confirmation isn't about what you do — it's about what God does in you. It isn't you "confirming" Christ; it is Christ "confirming" you with the Holy Spirit. The word confirmation means "an act of strengthening." In the sacrament of confirmation, the baptized soul is strengthened with the full outpouring of the Holy Spirit.

What is confirmation all about? According to Church teaching, it is about empowering you to live the Holiness Revolution. The Council of Trent teaches us that "The confirmed become stronger with the strength of a new power, and thus begins to be a perfect Solider of Christ!" Saint Thomas Aquinas tells us, "The sacrament by which spiritual strength is conferred on the one born again makes him in some sense a **front-line fighter for the faith of Christ."**

"Those who receive the Sacrament are more perfectly bound to the Church and are enriched with a special strength of the Holy Spirit. Hence **they are, as true witnesses of Christ, more strictly obliged to spread and defend the faith by word and deed."** (CCC 1285)

Confirmation fortifies us with the strength of God the Holy Spirit himself. By virtue of our confirmation, we have been sealed with the Holy Spirit and have sworn an oath to serve Christ the King as his soldiers. And as soldiers, we are called to spread and defend the Kingdom of God.

How do we spread the Kingdom of God? Naturally, we don't pick up arms and go off slaughtering foreign peoples in order to gain more territory. Instead, we strive to slaughter the sin that lies in the hearts of those we meet. In spreading the Kingdom of God, we are called to evangelize and to share the Good News of Jesus with as many people as we possibly can. If we have been given the greatest treasure, the treasure of Jesus Christ, we must share it with others. In this, I think of the Roman Empire. The ancient Roman Empire often conquered other lands and territories for the sake of spreading its kingdom. The reason the Romans wanted to spread their kingdom was because they were confident that they had the best way of life and that every person should live their way of life. Is this not the mentality we Christians should have? Shouldn't we consider living with Christ the King in the Kingdom of God the greatest way of life? And shouldn't we be eager to invite all peoples to live this great way of life? If we truly believe the words of Jesus ("The thief comes to steal, slaughter and destroy, but I have come so that you might have life and have it to the fullest." John 10:10), then how can we do anything but want to share this way of life with the world?

But not only does the Christian soldier spread the Kingdom of God; he must also defend the Kingdom of God. If we thought spreading the kingdom was difficult, just wait until we learn how difficult defending it can be. Defending the teachings of the Catholic Church is something that has become very countercultural. Think about the things the Church stands strong against: abortion, contraception, same-sex marriage, sex only within the sacred bond of marriage, relativism. These can be difficult teachings not only to understand and embrace, but even more so to defend. In order to defend the faith well, we must know it well. Scripture tells us to "Always be prepared to make a defense to anyone who calls you to account for the hope that is in you, yet do it with gentleness and reverence." (1 Peter 3:15)

The Holy Spirit equips the Christian with everything he needs to become a saint. The Holy Spirit equips the Christian with everything he needs to be a great disciple. The Holy Spirit equips the Christian with everything he needs to help bring about the Kingdom of God. The grace received by the Holy Spirit in confirmation is a grace of strength, *gratia ad robur,* which literally means "grace for the fight." **As revo-**

lutionaries, we have been given the grace to fight the good fight.

"Now to the King eternal, immortal, invisible, the only God, be honor and glory forever and ever. Amen. Timothy, my son, I give you this instruction in keeping with the prophecies once made about you, so that by following them you may fight the good fight, holding on to faith and a good conscience." (1 Timothy 1:17–19)

Prayer for Strength: *Come, Holy Spirit, in this time of need, strengthen me. You are my strength and my shield; you are my refuge and strength, a very present help in trouble. I know that your eyes go to and fro throughout the earth to strengthen those whose hearts long for you. The body grows weary, but my hope is in you to renew my strength. I do not fear, for you are with me. I am not dismayed or overwhelmed, for you are my God. I know you will strengthen me and help me; that you will uphold me with your righteous hand. Even as the shadows of darkness cover me, I feel the comfort of your strength. Amen.*

TALK ABOUT IT.

(If reading with a group, use these questions for discussion.)

1. Do you take the Eucharist for granted? Why or why not?

2. Are you afraid of going to confession? Why or why not?

3. Do you believe that confession can help you overcome your sins? Why or why not?

4. Do you see how the Catholic Church is the "blueprint for holiness?" Explain this in your own words.

5. Are there any teachings of the church that you struggle with? Talk about these issues together.

6. What kind of community do you have? Are your friends living for Jesus and striving to be saints? Do you need to stop hanging out with some of your friends and seek out other friendships?

7. What kind of strength do you need to ask the Holy Spirit for?

8. The fruit of the Holy Spirit is love, peace, joy, patience, generosity, kindness, faithfulness, gentleness, and self-control. Which fruits do you live well? Which could you grow in?

TAKE ACTION

ACTION STEP 1: Start going to daily Mass at least one day each school week before or after school. If you don't know daily mass times that would fit into your schedule, go to **www.masstimes.org.**

ACTION STEP 2: Go to adoration this week and spend an hour with Jesus in the holy Eucharist. To find adoration near you, visit: **http://www.therealpresence.org/chap_fr.htm**

ACTION STEP 3: Commit to praying the Rosary more often. Turn off the radio whenever you are in the car and pray the Rosary then, or pray it before you go to sleep.

ACTION STEP 4: If you need more Christ-centered friendships, write a prayer to Jesus describing to him the kind of friends you need in order to be holy.

ACTION STEP 5: Fold a piece of paper in half. On one side of the paper write down all the ways Jesus is asking you to spread the Kingdom of God. On the other side of the paper, write down the ways he is asking you to defend the Kingdom of God. Pray for the strength to live this.

ACTION STEP 6: Research confession times at local churches and commit to a monthly confession.

ACTION STEP 7: Start concluding each day before you go to bed with a quick examination of conscience reviewing your day and asking God to strengthen you to be better the next day.

www.Holness Revolution.com

PART THREE:

THE REVOLUTION OF THE WORLD

7
CALLED TO GREATNESS

"The world will offer you comfort, but you weren't made for comfort, you were made for greatness." (Pope Benedict XVI)

The last three chapters of this book are dedicated to helping you realize that you are called to greatness and helping you discern what this call looks like in your life.

The desire to be great is built into us. No one ever says, "I hope I'm a benchwarmer this year on the baseball team!" or "I really hope to make straight D's on my report card this year!" Of course not; this would be ridiculous. **Our hearts were created to desire greatness and to refuse to be ground down by mediocrity.**

Children dream of being the superhero who saves the world and protects the innocent. They dream of being brave cowboys and daring undercover cops. Young kids dream of being the pro football quarterback throwing the game-winning pass or the person singing in front of thousands. Children long to live their lives for something that matters. They long to be brought into a great adventure.

Not only do children dream of being great, but in their hearts they dream of goodness. They are much more likely to play the superhero saving the human race than the villain seeking to destroy humanity. They are more likely to play the cop that defends justice than the bank robber or the murderer. My daughter never pretends to be the Wicked Witch, but she never fails to want to be Dorothy fighting the Wicked Witch. Children dream of being cops and firefighters. They desire goodness.

God fashioned every one of us to desire greatness and goodness, but somewhere along the road of life, these childlike desires were crushed out of us. My dear brothers and sisters, if this desire for greatness has been crushed, I plead with you to pray earnestly for it to be restored. We must continue to embrace a childlike heart as teenagers and as adults. Adults so often stray from the call to greatness and move into a pathetic survival mode that tries to get them to tomorrow. Instead of living their call to goodness, so often adults end up living lukewarm lives that desire material wealth rather than justice.

We are not called to live a mediocre life — we are called to greatness. God doesn't want your life to be meaningless. He doesn't want you to go through the motions and live each day lacking passion and purpose. God wants you to share in his glory and to live the adventure of discipleship. He wants to do something amazing in and through you. The life of discipleship is meant to be a life of adventure. It's not supposed to be a drag.

KNOW YOUR WORTH

The reason so many Christians go through life never obtaining the greatness God wants to bestow upon them is that they don't know their worth. They don't know how amazing they are. The world and the Devil have crushed our childlike desire for greatness by telling us that we are worthless.

We have been told that our worth and sense of self-confidence should be wrapped up in what we do, but that isn't what the Lord tells us. The Lord tells us that **our worth comes from who we are, not what we do.** And who are we? "See what love the Father has bestowed on us that we may be called the children of God. Yet so we are. The reason that the world does not know us is that it did not know Him. Beloved, you are God's children now." (1 John 3:1–2a)

The reason the world judges everyone's worth on what they do is because the world does not know Christ. These people live for themselves as opposed to allowing Christ to live in them. "Man looks at outward appearance but the Lord looks at the heart." (1 Samuel 16:7)

The Lord doesn't care about how smart you are, how athletic you are, how musically inclined you are, how shy or how outgoing you are. The Lord is concerned with *who* you are. He is concerned with whose you are. You are the Father's beloved son with whom he is well pleased (Matthew 17:5; 2 Peter 1:17). As baptized Christians we share in Jesus's sonship. The Father sees us and adores us and loves us simply because we are his children.

I think about my own children, Sophia and Giovanni. Sophia is four and Giovanni is two. They are both so crazy and so full of energy. They are so strongwilled. Sometimes they can do things that drive me crazy! Sophia runs around in circles and never sits still. Giovanni stays awake late at night, refuses to take naps, and cries for hours at a time. They break things they aren't supposed to play with. They spill water all over the couch and juice all over the floor. The list goes on and on. Sometimes I look at other toddlers and wonder why they seem to be so much calmer than my crazy little duo, but at the same time, every second I see my little princess and every moment I look at my little man, I am so happy and so filled with love that they are who they are. Yes, Sophia's wild, but she's my precious baby girl. Yes, Giovanni is strongwilled and has an attitude, but he is my well-beloved son with whom I am well pleased. I love them not because of what they do or do not do; I love them simply because they are mine. Even amid their flaws, their daddy sees them as perfectly perfect. "I love you and you are mine." (Isaiah 43:2)

If a broken sinner like me can have such great love for his children, how much more does God the Father love us! We are his beloved children, and even though we are a handful and we don't always act like children of God, he still loves us because we are his. He loves us because of who we are. And who are we? We are his. Nothing you do will ever make your Father love you any more or less. Every second of the day, through all of your sins and shortcomings, your heavenly Father looks at you with eyes of adoration. He adores his child. You are precious in his sight because you are honored and he loves you (Isaiah 43:4).

Last year I ran into a high-schooler who was seriously struggling with her sense of self-worth. Her parents placed a lot of pressure on her and she felt that she couldn't ever live up to their expectations. Because of their pressure and because of the evil words and comments from the girls in her school, the only confidence she had was in her worthlessness. I asked her to do something for me; I asked her to start waking up every day and looking in the mirror and saying, "I am loved, because God made me out of love. I'm amazing, because God made me amazing." She assured me that although this would be extremely difficult for her to do, she would try. The next day she called me and said that she'd spent more than an hour standing in front of her mirror. She never got the words out. And so she tried the next day, and the next day. Over a period of a few months in daily prayer, she gradually was able to face the mirror and acknowledge her true self-worth.

You are amazing because God made you amazing. You aren't amazing because you're an incredible athlete. You aren't amazing because you're skilled at math. You are amazing because God made you amazing. No matter what you do or don't do, he made you amazing.

This simple phrase can become very powerful. Use it whenever you need it and replace the word *amazing* as needed.

I am amazing because God made me amazing.

I am important because God made me important.

I am beautiful because God made me beautiful.

I am valuable because God made me valuable.

I am worthwhile because God made me worthwhile.

I am loved because God made me out of love.

THE GOD OF TRANSFORMATION

Our heavenly Father wants to give us everything we need to achieve the greatness to which he is calling us. He is a God of transformation. He is a God who takes sinners and makes them saints, a God who takes the speechless and makes them prophets, a **God who takes the ordinary and makes them extraordinary.**

Just look at how the God of transformation has worked in the past. Throughout Scripture, God uses the broken. He finds the biggest rejects and fools he can and accomplishes amazing things through them.

He took Abraham, a man who was unable to have children, and transformed him into the father of many nations because of his faith.

He took Moses, a man who was unable to speak clearly, and transformed him into the mouthpiece for the Israelites and the proclaimer of the divine covenant.

The God of transformation took a little shepherd boy named David, a man who would later fall into the sins of murder and adultery, and he transformed him into the greatest King of Israel. This little shepherd boy successfully defeated all of the enemies of Israel and conquered new lands for his kingdom. He united the divided nations of Israel.

The God of transformation took Jeremiah, a teenager who was scared to speak, and made him a great prophet fearless of what others said.

He took Matthew, a sinful, tax-collecting thief, and made him a great evangelist.

He took Mary Magdalene, a prostitute and a shame to her people, and made her an example of purity and holiness.

The God of transformation took an ordinary fisherman named Peter, a man with limited knowledge and limited faith, and transformed him into the rock on which the Catholic Church was built. This fisherman became the first pope. He preached the Gospel and converted thousands upon thousands of people. He healed the sick and raised the dead.

The God of transformation took an ordinary teenage girl named Mary, born of a simple and poor family, and choose her to be the great Mother of God, the queen of heaven and earth, the queen of all disciples, the queen of peace.

The God of transformation took a persecutor of the early Christians named Saul, a man who ordered and witnessed shamelessly the first Christian martyrdom, and transformed him into Paul, the proclaimer of the Gospel to the Gentile world. This murderer became a great preacher. He built up the Church throughout the world. He authored many of the inspired texts of sacred Scripture. He opened the doors of the Church to the world.

The God of transformation takes ordinary men and women and transforms them into great saints. Read the lives of the saints. You will find that many of them were poor, simple, and uneducated. You will find that many of them were sinners, heretics, and harlots. The God of transformation took the ordinary and made them extraordinary.

But he proves his power even more. Every day, on every altar of the world, the God of transformation takes ordinary bread and wine and transforms it into his own body and blood. **He takes what is lifeless and makes it divine.** He takes what is worldly and makes it heavenly.

Now, let's be honest — if God can change bread and wine into his own divine being, how can we ever question whether or not he has the ability or the desire to transform our brokenness and use it for his glory?

If you are steeped in a life of sin, he wants to transform you into an extraordinary saint.

If you are broken and have been wounded by others, he wants to heal you in extraordinary ways.

If you are crippled by fear or lacking in trust, he wants to use you in extraordinary ways to bring about the Kingdom of God.

If you aren't smart enough, loved enough, or good enough, the God of transformation wants to prove his holiness through you. It pleases him to use the rejected, the broken, and the weak. He loves these people because **in their weakness he is glorified.**

Jesus takes ordinary men and women and transforms them into saints every day. This is what he can do, and this is what he wants to do in your life. Do you believe it? It's time for you to embrace your worth and stop making excuses!

God wants to use you to accomplish a great mission through you. He wants to use you to bring about a complete and radical change in this world. He wants to prove his holiness through you.

He wants to take you, who are ordinary, and use you for something extraordinary. God wants to use you in amazing ways! Will you let him? Will you let him make you great? Will you say yes?

Stop making excuses. Stop trusting in yourself and start trusting in him. You have what it takes because you have Christ.

You are called to greatness!

You are called to do great things for the Church!

You are called to sainthood!

GOTTA HAVE FAITH

In John 14:12, Jesus says to his disciples, "I tell you the truth, anyone who has faith in me will do what I have been doing, and he will do even greater things than these." Jesus turns water into wine, walks on water, calms the storms, multiplies the loaves and fishes, heals the sick, cures the blind, opens the mouths of the mute and the ears of the deaf, allows the lame to walk, casts out demons from the possessed, and he even raises the dead. Wow! What a list. Anyone who has faith in Christ will do greater works than these!

Now, if I were the average Christian, and if this were the average

Christian book, I'd follow the previous paragraph by telling you that Jesus doesn't want to work like this anymore. I'd say he doesn't actually mean that he wants to perform literal miracles through us, but rather that his modern-day "miracles" are seen when people share with others and lend a helping hand. I'd say we can "heal" people by listening to them and "multiply the loaves" by encouraging others to share. But I'm not the average Christian and this isn't the average Christian book.

As I said in the introduction of this book, we, the people of God in the third millennium, are living in an amazing time of salvation history. Pope Paul VI, Pope John Paul II, and Pope Benedict XVI have all prophetically spoken of a new Pentecost, a new evangelization, and a new springtime within the Church and throughout the world. The Holy Father is calling us to a revolution of holiness led by the Spirit of God. If this is a new Pentecost, then I am convinced that the Lord wants to use his servants like he does in the Acts of the Apostles after the first Pentecost.

We have lost the meaning of the word *miracle*. A miracle is an event in which the supernatural order overrides the natural order. For a miracle to happen, we need to have supernatural faith. We need to have complete confidence that God can and does still work in the lives of his people and that he wishes, more than anything, to manifest his glory to the world. The early apostles are an example of this supernatural kind of faith. In the Acts of the Apostles, the apostles preach the Gospel and convert thousands. They cure the crippled and the dying. They cast out unclean spirits. They are freed from prison by the angel of the Lord. They raise the dead.

If we are going to have any chance in succeeding in the revolution of holiness, the revolution of renewing the culture of death, then we need miracles. We need God to use us to raise to new life this culture that has died. We need God to heal those infected by materialism, individualism, pluralism, relativism, greed, lust, sloth, anger, pride, and vainglory. We need supernatural miracles to manifest that he—not we—is Lord over all.

Why did the apostles perform miracles after the first Pentecost, while we fail to do so during the new Pentecost? I think it is because they truly had supernatural faith and we simply do not. They had received completely the gift of the Holy Spirit and believed that the God who dwelled in them was greater than the evil in the world. Prior to the descent of the Holy Spirit, they were mere fishermen and tax collectors, but after, God proved his holiness through them as they spread Christianity to the ends of the earth.

If I am honest with myself, I so often fail to truly believe that Jesus Christ wants to accomplish a great work through me. I fail to believe that he is powerful enough to work through a fallen, sinful man like me. I hate to admit this, but so often I fail to believe that when I am praying for someone my prayers will be answered, in a miraculous fashion.

In Scripture, God says, "I will prove the holiness of my great name, profaned among the nations, in whose midst you have profaned it. Thus the nations shall know that I am the Lord, says the Lord God, when in their sight I prove my holiness through you." (Ezekiel 36:23) Often, I don't expect God to prove his holiness through me. I believe that God wants to and really can accomplish great and wondrous deeds, but I fail to believe that he wants to do this *through* me. I think, "There must be someone better, Lord. You want to renew the face of the earth, but you want to do it through someone else."

We need to have supernatural faith. We need to have the faith of a child.

A few years ago I had a middle school boy come to a summer camp I help run. Throughout the week of camp, we talked every day about the Blessed Mother Mary and the power of the Rosary. A few months later, this young man sat down at the dinner table with his family and heard some of the hardest news any person could hear. His mother had gone to the doctor because she wasn't feeling well and found out that her entire body was filled with cancer. She was to go back to the hospital the next morning for an emergency surgery that would hopefully save her life. The odds were against her. The young boy looked at his mom and dad, and asked if the family could pray a Rosary. For the first time ever, they did so as a family. The next day, his mother went to the hospital for the surgery. To her surprise, and to the utter shock of the doctor, the cancer was completely gone. There was not a trace left of the disease that had flooded her body the day before. Mary, Queen of heaven and earth, and Jesus Christ her Son, healed this woman because of the faith of a child.

I have heard countless stories like this, and yet, it is still hard for me to have faith. I always doubt. Lord Jesus, have mercy on me, a sinner. May our prayer be the prayer of our brother in scripture: "Lord I believe, help my unbelief." (Mark 9:25)

When we have faith, the God of transformation will accomplish the most amazing things through us.

TALK ABOUT IT.

(If reading with a group, use these questions for discussion.)

1. Do you desire greatness? Why or why not?

2. Do you know your worth? Or do you struggle to see yourself as good?

3. Do you take your identity in who you are or in what you do? Why is it important to take your identity in who you are instead of what you do?

4. If the God of transformation transformed you into the saint He wanted you to be, what would this life look like? What extraordinary things is he calling you to accomplish for him?

5. Do you have small faith or big faith? How can you increase in faith?

6. Spend some time sharing with one another miracles you have heard of happening. Do you believe that God wants miracles to happen in your life?

TAKE ACTION

ACTION STEP 1: If you are struggling to believe in your worth as a child of God, wake up every day and look in the mirror and say, "I am loved, because God made me out of love. I'm amazing, because God made me amazing."

ACTION STEP 2: Seek someone out who is struggling to believe in their worth as a child of God. Tell them how much God loves them and how amazing they are in the eyes of God.

ACTION STEP 3: Reach out to people you have ignored. Talk to them. Show them that they have dignity and are worthwhile. Spend quality time with them.

ACTION STEP 4: Start reading about the lives of the saints and how God transformed them to do amazing things for his kingdom. Go to **http://www.americancatholic.org/e-news/enews-letter-signup.aspx** and sign up to have free saint biographies emailed to you each day.

ACTION STEP 5: Seek out someone that has seriously hurt you in the past. Take time with them. Share with them how you have been hurt and tell them that you forgive them.

www.Holiness✝Revolution.com

8
LIVE THE ADVENTURE

Each summer, I help run a high-adventure summer camp for junior high and high school youth called Catholic Youth Summer Camp (cysc.com). Our mission at Catholic Youth Summer Camp is to provide a week of high-adventure activities that are used to propel the youth into a high-adventure relationship with Jesus Christ, the adventure of the sacramental life and mission of the Church, the adventure of faith, discipleship, and evangelization. We ride Jet Skis and go water tubing, we play paintball and go mountain boarding. We strap people inside of twelve foot tall inflatable hamster balls and roll them down a twenty-seven foot ramp. We throw kids into a mud pit and cover their bodies with paint. But ultimately, the real adventure we have at camp is living our faith well. Christianity is not passive. It's not inactive. There is absolutely nothing boring about our faith. The life of discipleship is the greatest adventure we could ever hope to live. When we answer God's call for our lives, we set out on the adventure of a lifetime and experience unforeseeable and unimaginable joy.

Imagine what the apostles and the saints must have thought while they were living the adventure God called them to live. I used to read the Bible and read about the lives of the saints and get frustrated. I would read and think about how exciting their adventure was and how amazing it must have been to live their life. Sooner or later, I heard God yelling at me: "Stop envying their adventure and start living your own!" The lives of the saints are amazing and inspiring, but they are no different than ours. We are called to the same radical holiness and radical mission that they were; the only difference is the saints said yes to God's adventure of discipleship and many of us have not. The saints were faithful in the small things and so God continued calling them to greater things.

You were created for a unique purpose, a unique mission, and a unique adventure to live. This chapter is dedicated to helping you discover your adventure, but ultimately, it is up to you to live it.

EVERY CHRISTIAN S ADVENTURE

So often I hear people talking about how the faith is boring or how their spiritual life is dry and lacking joy. So often I hear people say that they aren't getting anything out of our Catholic faith. The reason for this is as clear as day. If your faith is boring or dry, it's because you aren't living a life of radical discipleship.

In our modern world we have divided the call of Jesus into two parts. We think that some of us are called to seek holiness and some are called to seek mission. The modern mentality is, "I need to have a personal relationship with Jesus, and once this personal relationship is perfect and solid and 'fulfilling,' then I will start reaching out to others and sharing my faith." But that isn't the way Christianity works. Jesus doesn't just say, "Come follow me." He says, "Come, follow me, and I will make you fishers of men." If you are a follower of Jesus Christ, then you are also called to be a fisher of men.

Every Christian is called to the adventure of evangelization, the adventure of sharing your faith with the world. We've grown up in a Church in which people have forgotten what it means to be Christian. In the lives of many, **Christianity has become a completely selfish faith.** Instead of a Christian being one who lives and proclaims the Gospel of Jesus Christ, the modern Christian uses God for his or her own good: "God, what's in it for me? What can you do for me? How can you help me?" While it is true that the Lord Jesus wants to be with you and aid you in times of difficulty, it's not all about you. It's about him. It's about his kingdom. We love and serve God because he is God and he deserves our love and service. Remember that baptism called us to live the priestly, prophetic, and kingly mission of

Jesus Christ.

Pope Paul VI understood this mission well, which is why he wrote *Evangelii Nuntiandi* (Evangelization in the Modern World), calling all Christians to the task of evangelization.

"The command to the Twelve to go out and proclaim the Good News is also valid for all Christians." (13)

"We wish to confirm once more that the task of evangelizing all peoples constitutes the essential mission of the Church. It is a task and mission which the vast and profound changes of the present-day society make all the more urgent. Evangelizing is in fact the grace and vocation proper to the Church, her deepest identity. She exists in order to evangelize." (14)

If your faith is boring or dry, it is because you haven't yet started to share it with others. Going to Mass, praying daily, and going to religion classes but never actually evangelizing is like conditioning and working out for a sport but never playing any games. If your team only worked out and conditioned but never played, you'd get bored with that team pretty quick. If you pray and learn your faith but have no mission, then yes, you will be bored to tears. Holiness and mission go hand in hand. Discipleship is about following Christ and fishing for men.

The truest adventure, the greatest adventure, the adventure of the apostles and the early Church isn't merely the adventure of knowing Jesus personally. On the contrary, the apostles' adventure begins once Jesus leaves — once they are given the Holy Spirit in order to spread the Gospel and share in the mission of the redeemer.

In 1990, John Paul II wrote the encyclical *Redemptoris Missio* (Mission of the Redeemer). The title of the encyclical itself stirs me up just thinking about the mission of Jesus Christ, the redeemer of the world. How incredible, how awesome and adventurous is his mission! Let us for a moment ponder the mission of the redeemer: At the foundations of heaven and earth, God, out of pure love, creates Adam and Eve. They live in a beautiful paradise called the Garden of Eden, in perfect harmony and union with the Blessed Trinity and with all of creation. But of course, Satan lies and deceives them, and they fall into sin. This sin breaks their union with God, and ever since, mankind has carried the mark of that separation from God. Because of sin, mankind was doomed to be separated from God for all eternity.

But then comes the mission of the redeemer. God the Son, who has no beginning or end, becomes a mortal man, with a beginning and an end. The Creator of the world steps into the world. He steps onto the battlefield to take on the enemy himself. He becomes man in order to challenge sin and death once and for all and free us from its bondage.

A redeemer is one who purchases a slave's freedom. Our freedom from sin and death was purchased with the price of his blood. At the heart of the mission of the redeemer is the salvation of all souls. Jesus suffered, died, and rose from the dead, defeating sin and death so that we could be reunited with the Blessed Trinity for all of eternity. Christ conquered sin and death once and for all, and through the waters of baptism we share in Christ's victory. "Where, O death, is your victory? Where, o death, is your sting?" (1 Corinthians 15:55) And through the waters of baptism, we also share in the mission of the redeemer.

Read these beautiful opening words of *Redemptoris Missio:*

"The mission of Christ the Redeemer, which is entrusted to the Church, is still very far from completion. As the second millennium after Christ's coming draws to an end, an overall view of the human race shows that this mission is still only beginning and that we must commit ourselves wholeheartedly to its service. It is the Spirit who impels us to proclaim the great works of God: 'For if I preach the Gospel, that gives me no ground for boasting. For necessity is laid upon me. Woe to me if I do not preach the Gospel!' (1 Corinthians 9: 16) In the name of the whole Church, I sense an urgent duty to repeat this cry of St. Paul. From the beginning of my Pontificate I have chosen to travel to the ends of the earth in order to show this missionary concern. My direct contact with peoples who do not know Christ has convinced me even more of the urgency of missionary activity, a subject to which I am devoting the present encyclical. The Second Vatican Council sought to renew the Church's life and activity in the light of the needs of the contemporary world. The Council emphasized the Church's 'missionary nature,' basing it in a dynamic way on the Trinitarian mission itself. The missionary thrust therefore belongs to the very nature of the Christian life."

As Christians, we share in the mission of the redeemer, seeking and striving to aid Christ in his mission of the salvation of souls. No matter what job you are asked to do for the Kingdom of God, no matter what vocation you are called to live, you are called to share in the mission of the redeemer. What an honor it is to share in this great mission.

What an amazing adventure! This is the adventure of the first apostles, the adventure of all the saints, the adventure of Jesus Christ. This is every Christian's adventure.

Don't be deceived — this is not optional. If you are called to be a disciple, you are called to mission.

LIVE YOUR ADVENTURE

"Dear young people, the Church needs genuine witnesses for the new evangelization: men and women whose lives have been transformed by meeting with Christ, who are capable of communicating this experience with others." (Pope Benedict XVI)

The Lord invites us into his mission and his adventure, but of course, there is no adventure to be had if we do not accept this invitation. Living the adventure requires that we learn how to evangelize, how to communicate our experience with Christ to others. Evangelizing is something many are afraid of, but it is truly as simple as introducing people to the person whom you love, the person of Jesus Christ, and his bride the Church.

If we are ever to answer our baptismal call to evangelization, and answer this call well, we must have a clear understanding of what the word *evangelization* really means. On a most basic level, to evangelize means to proclaim the Good News that God became man in order to restore man's fallen and corrupt human nature (John 1:14). As Scripture clearly points out, "All have sinned and fallen short of the glory of God" (Romans 3:23) and "the wages of sin is death." (Romans 6:23) But "God proves His love for us that while we were still sinners, Christ died for us," (Romans 5:8) and in his perfect sacrifice on the cross and the new life we received in baptism, we have been set free from the chains of sin and death, brought into the family of God as co-heirs with the Son (Romans 8:17). In the mystery of the cross, we are offered freedom from sin and death, freedom from the empty promises of this world, freedom to live in love, and the freedom to spend all of eternity sharing the divine life of the Blessed Trinity. **Truly this is the Good News!** It is not decent news, nor is it average news, nor is it inconvenient news — it is *good* news. This is the best news anyone could ever hope to hear, and it is the best news you could ever hope to share.

If you want to be a revolutionary, you need to know how to evangelize. The problem we come across is that many Catholics do not know how. Here I give you eight elements to evangelization. Please understand that evangelization isn't an eight-*step* process. It isn't a formula to be followed. It is a dynamic process involving a number of key elements, in which the power and inspiration of the Holy Spirit lead. In order for you to be an effective evangelist, all eight elements need to be involved at different times and in different ways. Read them not as a list, but as different ministry skills that we should always be growing in and improving. You don't need to be perfect at the first element before you move on to the second. Instead, you should be growing in all eight elements at all times.

Element 1: Fall in love with Jesus

The first and most important step in evangelization is to fall in love with Jesus Christ. Saint Alphonsus Liguori said, "I love Jesus Christ, and that is why I am on fire with the desire to give him souls, first of all my own, and then an incalculable number of others." One cannot share what one does not have. If the love of Jesus is not alive and burning in our hearts, how could we ever expect to share this love with the world? Evangelization starts in your heart and the relationship you foster with Jesus through prayer and the sacraments. After your heart is flooded with love for Jesus, you will be able to share the overflow of your love with other people.

But the heart is not all that matters. The mind too is critical, which leads us to element two.

Element 2: Learn what you believe and why you believe it

For Saint Thomas Aquinas, this second element of evangelization seems to be a spiral of love. The more we know, the more we love, and the more we love, the more we seek to know (ST I–II, 27,2). If we do not know our beliefs and how to share them with others, not only will our evangelization suffer, but so will our love for Christ. Ultimately our love for Jesus is fueled and strengthened by our knowledge of the one who saves us.

Over and over again I get e-mails from teenagers who are faced with conversations about the faith with peers or even adults, and they have no idea how to defend what they believe. If we do not take studying our faith seriously and make it a priority in our life, when the time comes for us to defend what we believe, we will fall short.

"But sanctify Christ as Lord in your hearts, always being ready to make a defense to everyone who asks you to give an account for the hope that is in you, yet with gentleness and reverence." (1 Peter 3:15)

Element 3: Be a witness

Pope Paul VI teaches us that "the first means of evangelization is the witness of an authentically Christian life." (EN 41)

Above all, the Gospel must be proclaimed by our witness. We have all heard the phrase from Saint Francis of Assisi calling us to "preach the Gospel at all times, and when necessary, use words."

How you live your life will determine how successful you are in drawing souls to Christ. If you proclaim Christ but live for the world, then you do nothing but harm the building of the Kingdom of God. It could be argued that one of the greatest causes of atheism in the world today is Christians who proclaim one creed with their lips and live another with their lifestyle.

If you are walking the narrow path and living with the joy and love of the Holy Spirit, people will notice. If you live with hope while others despair, people will notice. If you live with faith while others doubt, people will notice. If you offer your suffering up as a living sacrifice, people will notice. If you place your happiness in heaven instead of in the material goods of this world, people will notice. If you defend truth while others fall prey to the waves of moral relativism, people will notice. If you love Jesus and live in the Spirit, people will see this and sooner or later, they will come to you, and they will ask you a very simple question: "What do you have that I don't have? What is the cause of your joy, peace, and love?"

You and I know the answer. It is Jesus.

Element 4: Tell them about Jesus

We must acknowledge that by itself "even the finest witness will prove ineffective in the long run if it is not explained, justified . . . and made explicit by a clear and unequivocal proclamation of the Lord Jesus." (EN 22)

What does this mean? It means that we must not only walk the walk, but we must also talk the talk. We should live in such a way that people ask us the reason for our joy, and when that door opens, we need to be ready to share the Gospel with them. If we are a great witness and live our faith well, but we never tell people about Jesus, we have missed an opportunity. This may mean that God is calling you outside of your comfort zone. This may mean the risk of rejection. This may mean stumbling over your words. But this is indispensable.

The most effective way to share your faith with another is through your testimony, your personal testament to what God has done and is doing in your life. People can argue about whether or not God exists using philosophy and biology and yada yada yada, but they cannot argue with your testimony. Nothing is more powerful than telling someone, "I know God exists because I have experienced his love." What is the doubter to say to that? He or she can't deny or reject your experience.

Again, people can argue and argue about the Resurrection and the factual truth of the Bible, but they can't tell you that you haven't encountered Jesus Christ in your own life. Share with them your own encounter with Jesus and what a relationship with him has done in your life. Share with them the freedom, the joy, the peace, and the hope that has resulted from your encounter with Christ.

Element 5: Have a sincere love for souls

I can't stress this element of evangelization enough. We must have a sincere love for every soul we encounter. It should cause you and me grief that so many souls are held captive to the lies of the Devil and the bondage of sin. When you walk down the street, when you walk through your school halls, when you walk through the mall, look at every person you pass and recognize that each has an eternal soul. Know that there is a real battle going on between the angels of the Prince of Peace and the angels of the Prince of Darkness striving to win that eternal soul. Love souls. If you don't love souls and you don't want to win them for the kingdom, then pray for this gift.

Evangelization is based on relationships. We build relationships with people so that we may bring them into a relationship with Jesus. We must sincerely care about each person and his personal salvation such that we are sharing the Gospel with him because we want to see him in heaven someday. The best people to evangelize and the most fruitful evangelization is with the people you build relationships with and share the Gospel with over time. When evangelizing, we should strive to understand the deepest desires of the individual's heart and show her how Christ is the fulfillment of those desires.

Element 6: Incorporate the individual into the community

After building a relationship with a person and sharing the Gospel with him, we need to invite him into the community of the faithful. It is simply impossible to have a relationship with Jesus without having a relationship with the body of Christ. The body of Christ strengthens us, nourishes us, and sustains us. Jesus wants every individual to have a personal relationship with him, but that's not enough; we also need to have a communal relationship with him, because without the Church, there would be no means for a personal relationship. The Church gives Jesus to us.

We can invite people into the community through social events at church, prayer groups, and youth groups. Ultimately, at some point these individuals should be invited to the sacraments such that their new life in Christ may be made complete. If they aren't baptized, we should invite them to consider this. If they aren't Catholic, we should invite them to consider becoming Catholic so they may receive the holy Eucharist. If they are Catholic, but have fallen away from their faith, we should invite them to reconciliation so they can be reunited with the faithful.

Notice how I use the word invite and not tell. You wouldn't invite a person to a party and not attend the party yourself. If you want to invite someone to youth group, don't just tell her about youth group, but pick her up and take her to it! If you want to get the person to confession, don't just tell her about confession, but pick her up and go to confession with her.

Element 7: Lead the individual down the narrow path

As a youth minister, I am always frustrated by youth group kids who invite their friend to youth group once, but then never bring him again. Time and time again I see youth group teens bring a friend, and their friend has an amazing time and the Lord starts working in his heart and speaking to him to change his life, but then the next week comes and the friend doesn't return. I'll ask my youth group teens why their friends didn't come back when they seemed to have such a great experience. They say, "I don't know," and so I reply, "Well, did you invite them again?" "No. I forgot."

We need to follow through! When evangelizing, we want to help people become mature Christians. Saint Paul says that we need to help others reach "the full stature of Christ." (Ephesians 4:13)

Initially, we want to meet a person where she is with the hope of raising her to the standards of Christ. Over time, we want to lead this person off the wide road that leads to destruction and onto the narrow path. We need her not only to have a radical turning away from sin, but she should also embrace a life of virtue and grace. A Christian should have a strong and active prayer and sacramental life. A Christian should also be incorporated into the Church's evangelistic mission.

You know you have succeeded in evangelizing a person when he is walking down the narrow path and starts evangelizing others. We evangelize to the extent that the ones we evangelize become evangelists themselves.

Element 8: Pray for the conversion of souls

This last element is the most important: Pray for the conversion of souls. It is not you and I who bring conversion, but only the Holy Spirit. We can do everything right and say the perfect words, but it is the Spirit of God who converts hearts. At the fundamental core of evangelization is an encounter with Jesus Christ. We as evangelist can aid in and help facilitate that encounter, but we can't force it. Ultimately, it is "the Spirit who calls out, 'Abba, Father'" (1 Corinthians 12:3) and the Holy Spirit who allows us to cry, "Jesus is Lord." (Galatians 4:6) The best thing we can do is entrust all souls to the love and mercy of Jesus Christ and the immaculate heart of Mary and trust that Christ will bring all souls to him.

One of my favorite prayers is the Chaplet of Divine Mercy. It is a simple prayer in which we beg Jesus over and over to convert sinners and to have mercy on the whole world. If you want to evangelize your family, your friends, or your school, start praying the Chaplet of Divine Mercy every day for them.

ALL FOR JESUS. ALL FOR HIS KINGDOM.

I have come to realize that the battle cry of the Holiness Revolution is "All for Jesus. All for his kingdom."

If our lives are meant to share in the mission of the redeemer, then all we do should be for Jesus. If our lives are meant to be about living a revolution of holiness, then all we do in life should be for his kingdom.

In order to live this battle cry, we need to change our mind-set. We need to see ourselves first and foremost as missionaries bringing Jesus to the world. **Everything in our life needs to be viewed as a share in Jesus's mission of building the Kingdom of God and bringing all souls to the Father.** The actions we perform, the things we do, the places we spend our time, the words we say, the sacrifices we make, the things we are praised for, the things we like and dislike in life need to be all for Jesus and all for his kingdom. The relationships with the people you interact with, the people you love, struggle to love, are annoyed and frustrated with, eat lunch and dinner with, those you are placed in class with — all need to be for Jesus and for his kingdom.

You are called to be an evangelist in all things and in all circumstances. You are called to be a missionary in all things and in all circumstances.

You may think, "But I don't have what it takes to build the Kingdom of God. I don't have the skills necessary to be a missionary. How am I going to handle that situation when one of my friends tells me they don't believe in God? How am I going to handle that situation when a friend tells me that their parents fight all the time and they blame God? How will I handle the rejection I'll experience when standing up for the truth? How will I explain why the Church teaches that abortion and homosexual marriage are wrong? How will I be joyful when I feel so depressed? How can I tell others about Jesus's love when I doubt it myself?"

The principle agent of evangelization, of missionary activity, of building the Kingdom of God is the Holy Spirit. On the one hand, we are amazing because we share in the redeeming work of Christ. But on the other hand, we are nothing because it is God alone who converts hearts. He doesn't need to use us; he chooses to use us.

Forget about asking how we will do it, and focus on being open to doing it. Remember, by right of baptism and confirmation, you have everything you need to accomplish the mission you have been given. If you are totally open, when the time comes, pray the simplest prayer we have, *Come Holy Spirit*, and he will take care of you.

DO WHAT YOU DO, AND DO IT FOR JESUS

Before we got married, my wife was working as a waitress at Cracker Barrel. She worked hard to get a theology degree and ended up working in a restaurant; nonetheless, she wanted to treat this job as a mission territory. Every day she would go into Cracker Barrel ready and willing to love every person she served as if they were Christ. My wife has this beautiful quality about her that when she looks at you and speaks to you, you feel engulfed in the love of Jesus. Month after month she engulfed her customers with the love of Jesus, but one day was special.

As she was serving a table with two older gentlemen, she shared her joyful spirit with them. One of the men was particularly cold. She recognized this, and affirmed in her heart her daily goal, just to make every person smile. So she did what she could. As the meal came to a close, with all sincerity, this man looked at my wife and said, "You are so happy. Why are you so happy?"

Startled by the questions, my wife smiled and said something frivolous.

Back in the kitchen, just moments later, she realized she had missed an opportunity to share the name of Jesus with someone! She prayed ardently, apologizing to Jesus for failing to tell this man about him and begging the Holy Spirit to open the door again before he left. And sure enough, as Amber was giving this man his check, he grabbed her hand and looked her in the eye and said, "Seriously, why are you so happy?"

"It is because I know Jesus, and I love him."

His friend, sitting across from him, said, "See?" Then and there, in the middle of a busy Cracker Barrel restaurant, this man began to tear up. He was a fallen-away Catholic who had left the Church after going through a rough divorce. My wife comforted the man, reassuring him of Christ's love and mercy, then left him in the care of what she knew must be a good Christian friend.

My wife always says, "Do what you do, and do it for Jesus." You don't need to look far to find mission territory. Your school is a mission field. Your place of work is a mission field. Your neighborhood and your sports teams are mission fields. Your family or your church may be a mission field. Do what you do and do it for Jesus. If you are an artist, use this for Jesus. If you are an athlete, do this for Jesus. If you are an actor or a singer or a dancer, do this for Jesus. Do what you are doing and figure out how you can bring Christ into that.

All for Jesus! All for his kingdom!

TALK ABOUT IT.

(If reading with a group, use these questions for discussion.)

1. Do you view living your faith as an adventure? Why or why not?

2. The chapter said: "If your faith is boring or dry, it is because you haven't yet started to share it with others." If your faith is dry, have you started sharing it with others?

3. Do you live in such a way that people will ask "what's different about you" or "why are you so happy?"

4. "For if I preach the Gospel, that gives me no ground for boasting. For necessity is laid upon me. Woe to me if I do not preach the Gospel!" (1 Corinthians 9: 16) Do you feel it is your necessity to preach the Gospel?

5. What do you find most difficult about evangelizing? Have you had any success in evangelizing others?

6. Who do you think the Lord has placed in your life to evangelize?

7. Do what you do and do it for Jesus. What do you do? How can you do this for Jesus?

8. What do you think your mission is?

TAKE ACTION

ACTION STEP 1: Write down a list of what you do (all your sports, extra-curricular activities, work, school, etc.) and then next to each thing, write down how you can do this activity for Jesus.

ACTION STEP 2: Pray about what special mission Jesus may be giving you. Write this mission down and hang it on your bedroom wall to remind yourself of it.

ACTION STEP 3: Start praying for the conversion of souls! I have found the Chaplet of Divine Mercy to be the best prayer for the conversion of souls. If interested, long onto **holinessrevolution.com** to learn how to start a Divine Mercy club at your school to start praying for the conversion of souls.

ACTION STEP 4: Write a list of ten people that you are going to reach out to and invite to some kind of faith based event. Five of the names should be people you have a close relationship with though they aren't really into their faith. The other five names should be people who are living lives of darkness that you know need the love of Jesus Christ. Start reaching out to these people. Be not afraid.

www.Holiness Revolution.com

9
THE REVOLUTION OF THE WORLD

The way the Holiness Revolution will spread throughout the world, the way the prophecy of the new evangelization and new Pentecost will be fulfilled, is through individuals answering God's call for their life. The Holiness Revolution isn't an organization or a group of people who join a club. It is Christians doing what they are called to do and renewing culture through individual and communal faithfulness to the Gospel.

A few months back, I met an amazing person. Brenda is an eighty-year-old woman who has been wheelchairbound for the past fifteen years because of multiple sclerosis. Her MS is so severe that she cannot move her legs, and she is barely able to move her arms. Her hands were stuck in a curled-up position and her body was as fragile as glass.

I was sitting in a coffee shop working on my computer planning the Holiness Revolution movement in Columbus. All of a sudden, I heard a woman praying loudly. She was praying for the people at the table next to me, offering up their families, their pains, their hurt, entrusting their lives to Jesus Christ. After she said amen, she made her way over to me in her motorized wheelchair. She came to me, in her complete brokenness of MS, and asked me if I would like prayers. I told her that I would love prayers for my beautiful wife and children and for all of you. Together, we prayed for you.

After this, I asked if I could pray over her. She prayed for continued faithfulness to her mission. After our time of prayer, I asked her how often she did this. Her answer surprised me.

"I do this every day. I ride through parks in the summer and down downtown streets. I ride through malls in the winter, and I pray with people."

"Do you ever get rejected?" I asked.

"I do. I've even encountered witches and atheists before who refuse to even look in my eyes. I get rejected about fifteen percent of the time, but eighty-five percent of the time I get to pray with people!"

This woman, an eighty-year-old, brittle, wheelchair-bound woman with MS, is a revolutionary. I asked her why she did this and do you want to know her answer?

"Jesus told me he wanted to bring a revival in this world, and so I prayed how someone as weak as me could help him bring this revival — and this is what he asked me to do. I can't do much, but I can do this!"

No matter how weak you may think you are, you are never too weak to be used in great ways by God. He wants to use the weak because in them he is made strong. He wants to prove his greatness through your littleness. **He wants to use you.** He wants to reveal your adventure to you.

I gave my life completely over to the Lord eleven years ago, and he has already called me on such great adventures! He called me to serve for a year as a missionary, where I traveled around with other missionaries in a twelve-passenger van, leading retreats daily for teens and sleeping in a different place every night. He has called me to appear on *Larry King Live* to debate about the infallibility of the Church. He has called me to appear on *The View* to share what God has done in my life. He has called me to talk about discernment on the *Today Show* with Matt Lauer. He invited me to be part of a five-week documentary called *God or the Girl*, which aired across the country allowing me to share what God has done in my life and about my discernment process to a huge audience. He has asked me to minister to women contemplating abortion. He has asked me to minister to teens contemplating suicide. He has asked me to minister to people enslaved to sin.

I am nothing amazing, but I can sit back and testify to the amazing things God has done through me. When I was nineteen years old, I randomly invited a few people over to my mom's house to pray. After an hour of prayer, we decided we should do this each week, and that we should invite others to do it. So the next week, we invited a few friends. Throughout the summer, we invited others and asked them to invite others. Within about eight weeks, we had more than seventy young people gathered in my mother's living room to listen to the Gospel preached and to pray together. We had to move out all the furniture and clear out space. As we prayed together, we lifted such a song of praise to the Lord that the police were summoned because of the "loud party" taking place. When the police arrived with a paddy wagon ready to arrest a bunch of drunken teenagers, my mother opened the door and invited them in to pray with us! She jokingly called these prayer meetings "Jesus Jams."

Within a year, the little prayer group that first started with five people in my mom's basement turned into a city-wide monthly prayer gathering of hundreds of high school students each month for Mass, preaching, and prayer. Throughout the years, Jesus Jams changed thousands of young people's lives. In these times of prayer, people were convicted of their vocation. People were called away to be missionaries. People left to become theologians. Youth groups formed in smaller parishes. The seeds of a revolution were started in the city of Columbus, Ohio. All of this came when I was but a teenager. "Do not say, 'I am too young.' To whomever I send you, you shall go; whatever I command you, you shall speak. Do not be afraid of them, for I am with you." (Jeremiah 1:7-8)

Jesus Jams no longer take place. The Lord is now working in different ways. But I am absolutely convinced that a mighty revolution is stirring in the city of Columbus because of what was started in my mother's basement and because of other great things the Spirit is doing in our city. I am absolutely convinced the Holy Spirit wants to stir up a mighty revolution in your city. I am absolutely certain he can use you to do this. You cannot be content with the way things are. You cannot use your youthfulness as an excuse. He wants you precisely because of your youthfulness. He wants you to discover your revolution!

DISCOVERING YOUR REVOLUTION

So often people ask me what they are supposed to do with their lives, what their adventure is, or how they are called to live the revolution of holiness. There is no way I can answer that question for you. In order to discover your revolution, you need to pray. If you aren't doing the Prayer Dare, you'll never discover your revolution, and you'll never live your adventure.

I think a lot of people mistakenly believe their adventure begins once they get their job or once they enter their vocation. If that were the case, the Church wouldn't give us the sacraments of baptism and confirmation until we got a job or until we entered our vocation. It isn't the priesthood or the married life that calls you to mission; it is baptism and confirmation. It isn't a job that calls you to mission; it is baptism and confirmation.

Following are some questions to help you discover your mission. Take these to prayer. Don't speed-read through this list. Spend time with it. Pray with it. These things can apply to discerning your vocation, but they can also apply to your state in life right now.

Identify the small things

We all want a great call. We all want to be asked by God to do something amazing. But people often want greatness without working for it. It would be crazy to think that an athlete would ever make it to the pros if he or she were lazy and sloppy in daily practice and conditioning. An athlete must be faithful in the small things in order to be called to big things. Jesus teaches us this same lesson in the parable of the talents when he says, "Well done, my good and faithful servant. Since you were faithful in small matters, I will give you great responsibilities. Come, share your master's joy." (Matthew 25:23)

If we are faithful in small matters in the spiritual life, then the Lord will bless us with great responsibilities in building the Kingdom of God. We must be faithful to him in the small matters of taking our daily prayer time, utilizing the sacraments, witnessing to the faith, and telling those around us about Jesus.

What are the small things he is calling you to? Are you doing these well? If you want to be a great servant of God but don't serve your family by doing dishes in the evening, chances are you will miss out on the great responsibilities in building the kingdom. Identify the small things God is calling you to do and strive to be excellent in those things. As you grow in the small things of loving and serving in day-to-day life, then the Lord will start putting bigger and greater opportunities before you.

Identify your passion

I fear that modern man is losing his passion. I pray that you have not lost yours. **I pray that you dream big dreams.** I pray that your heart is passionate for things that matter and not for the things of this world that fade away. So many people are passionate about material objects or about professional sports teams. Why would you waste your passion on an object? Why would you waste your passion on a group of twenty-two guys who throw around a pigskin? Is your deepest passion a video game or a musical artist? If so, dream bigger!

Look beyond the things of this world and ask yourself what you are passionate about in the Kingdom of God. Is it the poor and the marginalized? Is it the unborn? Is it those considering an abortion? Is it the elderly or the forgotten? Is it those who are rejected and unwanted, those suffering with depression and thoughts of suicide? Is it the disabled and the suffering? The sick and the dying? The agnostic and the confused? The atheist or the apathetic? The spiritually poor and depraved? Those from broken homes? Are you passionate about taking care of children? Are you passionate about teaching the faith? Are you passionate about leading others in prayer or preaching the Gospel?

What are your deepest desires? What is the truest longing of your heart? Often, coming to know the desires of your heart leads you to an understanding of God's will for your life. If you are passionate about the poor, chances are you are called to serve them in some way. If you are passionate about children, maybe you are called to serve in an orphanage or for the pro-life movement or as a mother or father. If you are passionate about helping others, maybe you are called to serve as a nurse or a doctor. If you are passionate about preaching, maybe you are called to be a priest. If you are passionate about listening to others, this may be a call to the priesthood, the religious life, or a job as a psychologist.

If you don't have passion, pray for it!

Identify your talents

Often you are passionate about the things you are good at. So spend time asking the Lord to reveal your gifts and talents to you. What are you good at? What gifts and talents has the Lord given you? What have others pointed out as your strengths? How can you use these gifts to serve others?

Jesus created us with our adventure in mind. The gifts and the talents he gave us can be vehicles to serve him and his people. But we need to be creative with this. Saint John Bosco loved magic and sports, and he used both as a means of evangelizing young boys. I have a buddy who loves martial arts and has been using this to teach people about the virtues. There is a great doctor in Columbus who is very talented in his profession and has used it to help so many women get pregnant who otherwise could not, and has preached against contraception to his colleagues no matter the persecution.

Often the Lord uses our talents to call us, but not always. Remember that he called Moses, who was a horrible speaker, to be the voice defending the Israelites. Just because you may not see something as a talent doesn't mean he won't call you in that direction. Be ready for anything!

Identify the need around you

Don't close your eyes to the countless needs around you. If you see a need, maybe you are the one called to respond to this need. If people suffering with depression always seem to come to your attention, maybe you are called to reach out to them. If people who are hungry are always standing on your street, maybe it is you who are called to feed them. If people near you are ignorant of their faith, maybe it is you who are called to teach them. If people around you are sinning through drugs and alcohol, maybe it is you who are called to preach against this in big and small ways. If people in your school are struggling with purity, maybe you are called to start a purity club.

What is the need around you? What is the pain you see? What is the bondage to sin you see? What is the despair you see? If you see the need, chances are it is the Holy Spirit who has opened your eyes. Chances are it is the Holy Spirit who is going to enable you to fulfill this need!

Identify your mess

One of the best phrases I have ever heard comes from a ministry friend of mine, Justin Fatica. He is a preacher revolutionizing the world by helping people everywhere realize how much they are loved by Jesus and how important it is to love like Jesus.

He likes to tell people, "Turn your mess into your message," meaning, use the word of your testimony to do great things. What is your past? This is a tough question, but it often teaches us how we can serve effectively. If you came from a broken or an abusive family, maybe the Lord is calling you to reach out to those who are struggling with the same thing. If you were addicted to pornography, maybe God is calling you to reach out to those who are still addicted. If you were raped, maybe God is calling you to help those suffering from a similar experience. If you had an abortion, maybe God is calling you to reach out to women who are considering an abortion. This is a matter of using your testimony to help others.

Your mess can be big or small things. If your mess was wasting too much time watching TV and being lazy, maybe your message is about doing something great with your life. If your mess was having a low self-worth, maybe your message is about telling others how much they are loved by their Father in heaven.

What's your mess? Just like Jesus can take the mess of the crucifixion and bring about the Resurrection and the salvation of souls, he can take the mess of your life and bring about freedom and salvation to souls.

Identify how you can be countercultural

You'd be amazed at how simply walking down the narrow path and being countercultural will reveal to you what God is asking of you. When you reject the things of this world, God opens your eyes to a whole new world. You start seeing things differently. You start realizing that there is more to life than selfish ambition. You start wanting to live for the Kingdom of God and not the kingdom of the world, the flesh, and the Devil.

Look at the culture you're living in and identify how you can be countercultural.

Here are some ideas:

- **Throw away your iPod.** Our culture is so noisy; the modern young adult is always surrounded by some kind of noise. The best thing I ever did for my prayer life was turn off my car radio. Whenever I drive, I drive in silence. The car has become a chapel for me, and honestly, it is now one of the primary places where God speaks to me. Sometimes when I am at work and in need of inspiration, I get in my car and drive, because I am sure I will hear God's voice in my chapel on wheels.

- **Give away fifty percent of your clothes.** Saint John the Baptist says that if you have one coat, give one away (Luke 3:11). Why do we act like he was joking? I dare you to simplify your life. Give to the poor not a few of the shirts you don't like, but fifty percent of your wardrobe. Imagine if we were faithful in this respect how much God would start speaking to us! We wouldn't be thinking about our possessions so much, but instead, we'd be thinking of giving ourselves to others. This one action may be what you need to move from selfish to selfless.

- **Stop watching TV.** It's amazing how much time we can give to meaningless entertainment. Imagine if in the evenings instead of watching TV, you spent that time doing something to build the Kingdom of God. Maybe you could pray the Rosary for the conversion of your school. Maybe you could write letters to your classmates one by one telling them about how much Christ Jesus loves them and why you hope they will love Jesus in turn. Your time is a gift from God — use it well!

Identify your cross

When I was discerning my vocation between the priesthood and the married life, my vocation director asked me to build a cross and carry it on a twenty-two-mile pilgrimage. Initially, I thought this was a ridiculous idea, but it proved to be the key to my vocational discernment. I built a large, eighty-pound cross and with a few of my friends, I set out on my pilgrimage. In two days I carried this cross in ninety-degree weather. If was so hot and the cross was so heavy that as I walked, the asphalt was literally melting under my feet. We started and ended our pilgrimage with the Sacrifice of the Mass. The entire time I carried the cross, my brothers prayed rosaries, novenas, chaplets, etc., as they walked by my side. On occasion, trying to walk up hills, I would need their help. I would depend on them. (To watch my experience of carrying the cross, visit my youth tube page "HolinessRevolution" or order the documentary "God or the Girl" from amazon).

After all of this my shoulders were bruised and bloodied, but I learned the key to discernment. The question of discernment is the question of your cross. During and after this experience, instead of asking God what he wanted from me, I started to ask him how he wanted me to die to myself.

Our adventure, our revolution, our vocation is a call to the cross, a call to lay ourselves down in humble service to others. Once I learned this lesson, my vocation was as clear as day to me. While I was inspired and humbled by the call of the priesthood, I knew God wanted me to lay my life down in humble service to a wife and children. I knew this would be hard for me and would require me to kill a lot of the selfishness inside me. I knew this was the cross I was being asked to carry.

Don't run from the cross Jesus is asking you to carry. If that cross means sacrificing the good of marriage for the sake of the priesthood or religious life, then carry that cross! If that means sacrificing your career dreams for the sake of being a missionary, then carry that cross! If that means sacrificing hard-earned possessions for the sake of the poor, then carry that cross! If it means sacrificing your time, your preferences, your comfort level, your weaknesses, then sacrifice it and carry the cross he extends to you.

Identify something risky, and do it

All our life our parents and teachers have told us to be safe. The result is a generation of wimpy Christians who don't want to do anything risky for the Gospel.

Saint Louis de Montfort once wrote, **"If we do not risk anything for God, we will never do anything great for Him."**

Brothers and sisters, God will not do anything great in and through you amid the comforts of your daily life. Take a risk. Maybe that means after graduating high school or during college you take a year off to do mission work (check out netusa.org). Maybe that means spending a summer in a third world country serving the poorest of the poor. Maybe it means deciding to visit different convents around the country. Maybe it means just entering the seminary or the convent and seeing what happens. Maybe it means deciding to be homeless for a summer and living on the streets praying with the homeless.

What scares you? Does mission in the third world scare you? Then do it! Does talking to the homeless on the street scare you? Then do it! Does telling your best friends about Jesus scare you? Then do it! Does starting a pro-life club in your school scare you? Then do it! Does praying the Rosary outside an abortion clinic or a strip club scare you? Then do it! Stop being so safe and do something great for the Gospel!

Identify something risky and do it. The apostles must have thought Jesus was insane when he told Peter to get out of the boat in a storm and walk on water. But that was Jesus's call. And Peter listened. Yeah, moments later he was drowning, but at least he listened. We always assume that Peter messed up, that it was his lack of faith that made him fall into the water. But maybe he didn't mess up. Maybe the only faith Jesus wanted of him was to get out of the boat and stop living the life of a fisherman so that he could start living a different life. Maybe Jesus wanted him to take the risk and actually start drowning. Why? Because while Peter was drowning, he cried out to Jesus and Jesus saved him. Maybe Jesus just wanted to show Peter that he had the power to save.

Don't think I'm not talking to you. This applies to you!

"If we do not risk anything for God, we will never do anything great for him."

Trial and error

The last thing to say is that you aren't called to only one adventure. In your youthfulness, try as many different faith adventures for Christ as you can. The building of the Kingdom of God is a very large task with a lot of different ministries and missions out there. Try different slippers on and if the shoe fits, then stick with it!

"Seek first the Kingdom of God and His righteousness, and all these things will be given you besides. Do not worry about tomorrow; tomorrow will take care of itself." (Matthew 6:33–34)

THE HEART OF REVOLUTION

"Love is the only force capable of transforming the world." (Pope Benedict XVI)

My dear brothers and sisters, at the heart of the Holiness Revolution, at the heart of everything we are about, there is one simple word: love. This Holiness Revolution will be nothing more than a passive stirring up of emotions if love is not at the heart of it.

The revolution of our hearts is about bringing love himself into our own lives.

The revolution of the world is about sharing love himself with the entire world, one person at a time.

We are called to abide in the rich love of Jesus Christ and then to take this love into the world.

Let me remind you what was said earlier: The perfect image of love is the outpouring gift of self found on the crucifix. Love is not a stirring up of emotions; **love is a sincere gift of self.** Love is a sacrifice. Jesus Christ sacrificed his own life on the cross for the ransom of souls. His sacrifice meant our gain. If we are to be revolutionaries of the love of God, can we expect anything other than the call to live the same sacrificial love of Jesus Christ?

"Whoever wishes to come after me must deny himself, take up his cross, and follow me. For whoever wishes to save his life will lose it, but whoever loses his life for my sake will find it." (Matthew 16:24–25)

In order for this revolution to mean anything, you will need to die to yourself and live a self-giving life of love.

John Paul II once wrote that "the Church of the first millennium was born of the blood of the martyrs" *(Tertio Millennio Adveniente, 37)* and that the Church was sustained in the second millennium from the spiritual martyrdom of the Religious. In speaking of the present-day Church, the Church of the third millennium, he indicates that the Church needs to be reborn by the spiritual martyrdom of those revolutionaries willing to lay everything down in service to the Lord and his Church.

This may be the strangest way to end a book, but I close with one simple prayer, the prayer that has been in my heart the entire time while writing:

> *Lord Jesus, I come before you and I beg that you will give the person who has read this book the grace to die. I pray for their spiritual martyrdom, that they might serve you without reserve, whatever the cost! Let them die, oh Lord! Let them die!*

"Here I am, Lord! I am ready! Send me!" (Isaiah 6:8)

TALK ABOUT IT

(If reading with a group, use these questions for discussion.)

1. Do you believe that even though you are young, Jesus wants to accomplish great things through you? Do you use your youthfulness as an excuse? Are you waiting until you are older to start living your adventure?

2. What are the small things he is calling you to? Are you doing these well?

3. What are you passionate about? How can you use this passion for building the Kingdom of God?

4. What are your gifts and talents? What do you think these reveal about God's mission for you?

5. What's the need around you? How can you be at service to this need?

6. What's your mess? How can you turn your mess into your message?

7. What's something counter-cultural that you can do to help you hear what mission Jesus is calling you on?

8. What cross is Jesus asking you to carry? How does he want you to lay your life down in service to others?

9. Do you play it safe out of fear or laziness? What is something risky you can do for Jesus?

10. After reading this book, how is Jesus asking you to die? How is he asking you to love? What's your mission?

TAKE ACTION

ACTION STEP 1: Write someone a letter and point out their gifts and talents and share with them how you want them to use those gifts for Jesus. Give them ideas on how they can do this.

ACTION STEP 2: Search Google for "St. Therese Sacrifice Beads." Research what these special sacrifice beads are and make a set for yourself. Each day, count the number of sacrifices you can offer up out of love for others.

ACTION STEP 3: Write a list of your passions, gifts, and talents. Then, prayerfully ask Jesus what mission you think he is calling you on. Take this list and mission to Jesus in adoration and leave it before the monstrance entrusting your mission to Jesus.

www.Holiness Revolution.com

ABOUT THE AUTHOR

Dan DeMatte challenges young men and women of today to live a life of radical holiness – A holiness that produces saints, not mere mediocre Catholics. Dan is married to Amber Marie and together they have three beautiful children. Dan is a Youth Minister, national speaker and retreat leader, and program director for a high adventure youth camp (Catholic Youth Summer Camp) aimed at drawing young people into the adventure of their Catholic faith. He starred in A&E's reality TV show, *God or the Girl,* he defended the Church and the Priesthood on *Larry King Live* and *The View,* and he has shared his testimony on the *Today Show.*

You can email Dan DeMatte at: **Dan@HolinessRevolution.com**

Join the Holiness Revolution
and learn how to bring the
Revolution to your city,
your parish, and your school at
www.HolinessRevolution.com

DECISION
point

THE DYNAMIC CATHOLIC
CONFIRMATION EXPERIENCE

"I am convinced this is the best invitation to young Catholics to accept and live their faith that I have encountered."

— CARDINAL DONALD WUERL, Archbishop of Washington

REQUEST YOUR FREE* PROGRAM PACK
at DynamicCatholic.com/Confirmation

The complimentary program pack includes: the complete DVD series containing 72 short films, the student workbook, and the leader guide.

*Just pay shipping.

DynamicCatholic.com
Be Bold. Be Catholic.

NOTES

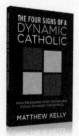

NOTES

NOTES

NOTES

THE
DYNAMIC CATHOLIC
INSTITUTE

[MISSION]

To re-energize the Catholic Church
in America by developing world-class
resources that inspire people to
rediscover the genius of Catholicism.

[VISION]

To be the innovative leader in the
New Evangelization helping Catholics
and their parishes become
the-best-version-of-themselves.

DynamicCatholic.com
Be Bold. Be Catholic.®

The Dynamic Catholic Institute
5081 Olympic Blvd
Erlanger, Kentucky 41018
Phone: 859-980-7900
Email: info@DynamicCatholic.com